MW01204895

PRESIDENTS
AT
PLAY

PRESIDENTS
AT
PLAY

George Sullivan

WALKER AND COMPANY
New York

First published in the United States of America in 1995 by Walker
Publishing Company, Inc.

Published simultaneously in Canada by Thomas Allen & Son Canada,
Limited, Markham, Ontario

Library of Congress Cataloging-in-Publication Data
Sullivan, George.
Presidents at play / George Sullivan.
p. cm.
ISBN 0-8027-8333-3 (hardcover). —ISBN 0-8027-8334-1 (reinforced)
1. Presidents—United States—Recreation—Juvenile literature.
[1. Presidents—Recreation.]   I. Title.
E176.8.S85   1995
973'.099—dc20   94-15002
CIP
AC

BOOK DESIGN BY GLEN M. EDELSTEIN

Printed in the United States of America

2   4   6   8   10   9   7   5   3   1

CONTENTS

ACKNOWLEDGMENTS

Many people contributed background information or provided photographs for use in this book. Special thanks are due Gary Walters, chief usher, Executive Mansion, the White House; Marlin Fitzwater, press secretary to President George Bush; Mary Finch, National Archives; Cyndy Bittinger, Calvin Coolidge Memorial Foundation; David J. Stanhope, Jimmy Carter Library; Kathleen A. Struss, Dwight D. Eisenhower Library; Kenneth G. Hafeli, Gerald R. Ford Library; Jim E. Detlefsen, Herbert Hoover Library; E. Philip Scott, Lyndon Baines Johnson Library; Steve Branch, Ronald Reagan Library; Mark Renovitch, Franklin D. Roosevelt Library; Pauline Testerman, Harry S. Truman Library; Katherine L. Brown, Woodrow Wilson Birthplace; and Bob Kinney, U.S. Military Academy, West Point. The author is also grateful to Francesca Kurti, TLC Labs; Herman Darvick; Bruce Pluckhahn; Brian Kathenes; Bert Botter; and Tim and Frances Sullivan.

CHAPTER 1

ON THE RUN

IT IS 6:05 A.M. ON A LATE-SPRING MORNING IN WASHINGTON, D.C. The sky is overcast, the temperature in the mid-sixties. Pennsylvania Avenue in front of the White House is quiet and empty.

At the White House press room, reporters, photographers, and television technicians are beginning to gather. "It's gray," says a TV producer. "Maybe he won't go."

"Are you kidding?" a photographer answers. "NBC is doing their 'Day in the White House' today; he'll jog."

Sure enough, at 6:50, the press pool is told to go to the South Lawn, in back of the White House. The president's limousine and a motorcade of a dozen cars and vans are waiting.

Moments later, President Bill Clinton emerges from the Executive Mansion. He is wearing blue shorts, a red T-shirt, a blue baseball cap decorated with gold leaf, and custom-made New Balance 997 running shoes with the words "Mr. President" stitched on the sides. Running with him this day are three first-term members of the House of Representatives, including Cynthia McKinney of Georgia and Representative McKinney's press representative.

Clinton gets into his limousine. Everyone else rushes for the cars and vans.

The motorcade eases out onto the city streets and heads south and east toward Hains Point, a park several miles from the White House, where today's run is to begin. The press vans keep blocks ahead of the president and the other runners. From time to time, photographers get out to take pictures of the group.

The president has long legs, a long stride, and a great deal of running experience. During the three-mile jog, he moves easily, often serving as a tour guide, pointing out historic sites, such as Fort McNair, where, as the president notes, those involved in the plot to assassinate President Abraham Lincoln were hanged.

President Clinton jogs about five days a week. He is a night owl who usually gets to sleep around midnight, is up by six A.M., and is out jogging not long after, although no one knows exactly when he will begin. He jogs in the heat and the cold, in the snow and the rain.

Nobody knows in advance where the president will go. He might take his limousine and begin at Hains Point. Other times he leaves the White House and jogs south, taking a sharp left turn at the Washington Monument and then running along the Mall to Capitol Hill. Sometimes he runs up the steps of the Capitol to build his leg strength.

On other occasions, the president runs in the opposite direction — on Pennsylvania Avenue west to Georgetown and the college he attended, Georgetown University. On one such run, a woman rushed up to the president, kissed him

President Clinton on an early-morning jog in Washington, D.C. A Secret Service agent stays close by. (WIDE WORLD)

enthusiastically, then jogged off, leaving Clinton with lipstick on his face.

No matter what route he takes, President Clinton seldom jogs alone. He runs with senators, members of the House of Representatives, governors, and mayors. He runs with old friends and new, educators, doctors, and TV or movie celebrities. When he ran with singer Judy Collins, she got winded and had to ride in the limousine.

Clinton had been in office only a month or so when construction began on an oval running track on the South Grounds adjacent to the White House driveway. Made of recycled automobile and truck tires, the track is almost a quarter mile long. It cost $30,000, with the money coming from private donations.

The construction of the track was the subject of news stories in leading newspapers and short features on network TV news programs. So much attention disturbed White House officials. "The American people believe this is reasonable," said a White House spokesperson in defense of the track. "And they think this is perfectly acceptable that the president have a place to run without leaving the grounds." But even after the track was built, Clinton continued to run in Washington streets or parks, using the track only for wind sprints at the end of his run.

President Clinton's official biography says that he started running in 1971 at the urging of his wife, Hillary Rodham Clinton, when the two of them were at Yale Law School. But boyhood friends of the president say that he was jogging as early as 1968, when he went to Oxford University as a Rhodes scholar.

The sporting life a president chooses often becomes a symbol of his administration and the times. Bill Clinton typifies the millions of Americans who seek to keep fit by pursuing a fairly rigorous running schedule.

President Ronald Reagan loved visiting his ranch in the mountains above the Pacific Ocean, northwest of Los Angeles. Photographs taken there of Reagan smiling on horseback helped to establish the feeling of trust and confidence people had in him.

One of Jack Kennedy's favorite sports was sailing. Pic-

A one-lane jogging track, made of recycled automobile and truck tires, was built for President Clinton on the South Grounds of the White House. (WIDE WORLD)

President Clinton unlimbers for a run by doing some toe touches. (WIDE WORLD)

tures of him aboard his boat, appearing relaxed and confident, his bushy hair being ruffled by the wind, his attractive wife at his side, helped to lend a romantic and vigorous image to his administration.

Fitness never seemed to be on the mind of William Howard Taft, the twenty-seventh president, who served from 1909 to 1913. Taft, who weighed more than 300 pounds, was so large that when he stayed at Abraham Lincoln's old guest house in Vermont, he couldn't fit on the bed and had to sleep on the floor. In those days, most people saw nothing wrong with being overweight. Eating well was a sign of good health and manliness.

A 300-pound candidate would have trouble getting elected today. Americans have come to associate fitness with being productive and successful. Candidates seeking votes try to show they're in good shape.

Taft and most other American presidents would have had a hard time keeping up with George Bush, who occupied the Executive Mansion until defeated by Clinton in the election of 1992. Bush seldom encountered a sport he didn't like. He played golf and tennis. He fished and hunted. Soccer, softball, and horseshoes were also on his agenda. And, like Clinton, Bush was an enthusiastic jogger. In fact, within a few days of his inauguration, Bush was out for a run. Dressed in bright orange running pants and a gray long-sleeved sweater, Bush chose Fort McNair, a District of Columbia army base several miles southeast of the White House, as his jogging site. Bush also jogged at the Naval Observatory in northwestern Washington. The Secret Service was happy with these sites. It was easier to protect the president at Fort McNair or the Naval Observatory than along city streets.

Bush ran about three miles a day, whenever his schedule

Like Bill Clinton, George Bush was an enthusiastic runner. Here he jogs with a group in Houston in 1991. (WIDE WORLD)

permitted. He took up jogging in 1976, after becoming head
of the Central Intelligence Agency, the CIA. Said Bush:
"Unlike many who say they've never seen a happy jogger, I
really enjoy it. It gives me time to reflect, to clear the head."

In 1984, when Bush was serving as Ronald Reagan's vice
president and seeking reelection, he faced Geraldine Fer-
raro, the Democratic vice-presidential candidate, in televised
debates. Before each debate, Bush practiced his answers
while jogging. And he did his running on a track that took
two minutes to get around—the same amount of time debate
participants were to be allotted for their answers.

Bush usually jogged indoors using a treadmill, a moving
belt whose speed he could easily control. When traveling, he
sometimes borrowed or rented a treadmill for use in his hotel
room.

President Nixon jogged indoors, too. But he didn't bother
with a treadmill. Nixon simply jogged in place in his White
House bedroom every morning.

Jimmy Carter was another jogger, and a very serious one.
Carter, who was a cross-country runner as a freshman at the
U.S. Naval Academy, ran as much as seven miles a day, and
forty to fifty miles a week.

President Carter called jogging "one of the high points of
my day," adding: "I start looking forward to it almost from
the minute I get up. If I don't run, I don't feel exactly right.
I carry a watch, and I can click off a mile in six and a half
minutes when I really turn it on." But "turning it on" once
almost caused a calamity.

One mid-September Saturday in 1979, Carter, along with
some 750 other runners, entered a ten-kilometer race in the
Catoctin Mountains, near Camp David, the presidential retreat. The distance of 10,000 meters, or ten kilometers—

10K—is equivalent to 6.2 miles. Carter had run that distance several times in the past, always timing himself. His best previous time for the distance was fifty minutes. On the day of the race, he planned to push himself in an effort to cut three or four minutes off his record.

Carter arrived at the starting line a few minutes before the race got under way. He wore a yellow sweatband around his forehead, the number 39, black socks, blue running shoes, and a gray T-shirt that announced: "Chairman of the Board." The gun sounded and the tightly packed swarm of men and women charged across the starting line and into the Maryland hills.

In the early stages, the road was mostly downhill, and Carter moved at a good clip. When the course led up a steep hill, Carter's running became labored. Then he turned pale and began to wobble and moan a little.

Dr. William Lukash, the president's physician, who was running with him, recognized that Carter was suffering from heat exhaustion and was near collapse. He urged the president to drop out of the race. At first, Carter protested, saying he wanted to continue. But Dr. Lukash insisted that the president "take a breather."

Secret Service agents who also had entered the race assisted Carter to a nearby support vehicle, where he was given oxygen. Then they helped him into his limousine and he was sped to Camp David, about a quarter of a mile away.

There Dr. Lukash administered standard treatment for heat exhaustion. Carter received about a quart of salt water through a vein in his arm. His body was also cooled by towels to help bring his temperature down.

Carter recovered quickly. About two hours after he had dropped out of the race, he appeared at an awards picnic

President Jimmy Carter, trailed by his physician, Dr. William Lukash, jogs on the South Lawn of the White House. (WIDE WORLD)

Exhausted by the heat, President Carter nearly collapsed in a race near Camp David in 1979. (WIDE WORLD)

and ceremony to present a trophy to the race's winner, Herb Lindsay. Asked how he felt, Carter smiled broadly and gave the crowd a thumbs-up sign. "I feel great! I pressed myself too much. But they had to drag me off," he said, grinning. "I didn't want to stop."

Later Dr. Lukash told reporters that at no point did he feel as if the president's life was in danger. But on the day after the race, a Sunday, photographs of Carter looking exhausted and ashen-faced appeared on the front pages of newspapers and on television news broadcasts. They jolted the American people.

Despite the incident, Carter gave no thought to quitting jogging. In the years that followed, running continued to be an important part of his physical fitness program. And as Carter approaches seventy years of age, he is still running three times a week, averaging three to four miles each time. He also enjoys tennis, skiing, and early-morning bird-watching excursions.

While presidents before the time of Jimmy Carter rarely ran for health and relaxation, many of them at least walked for fitness. Harry Truman, for example, was well known for the daily walks he took. He would set out from the White House at seven o'clock in the morning for an enthusiastic two-mile constitutional, parading along at the brisk pace of 120 steps a minute. His Secret Service men scrambled to keep up. On trips to other cities and during family vacations, Truman stuck to the routine. Dr. Wallace H. Graham, Truman's physician, once said: "Mr. Truman was in better condition when he left the White House than when he entered it, and, in my opinion, walking had a lot to do with it."

During his first several weeks as president, Truman was able to travel along streets near the White House and hardly

Accompanied by a Secret Service agent, President Harry S. Truman takes a morning stroll in Chicago in 1950. (HARRY S. TRUMAN LIBRARY/ CHICAGO *DAILY NEWS*)

be noticed. But once local newspapers started to feature stories about his morning jaunts, throngs of sightseers began to watch for the president and then trail along after him. Reporters and newspaper photographers joined the mob. Truman tried to outwit the gawkers by changing his route and time of departure, but it was useless.

Truman eventually came up with a solution to the problem. He would have his black limousine travel to different locations on the outskirts of Washington. Once he arrived in a suitable neighborhood, he would get out and enjoy his walk in peace.

Most earlier presidents who sought to walk in Washington had none of Harry Truman's problems with the public. William Henry Harrison got up early to do his own marketing, buying chops or steaks for breakfast. Zachary Taylor was another president who did his own shopping, holding friendly conversations with local farmers. Abraham Lincoln also liked to rise early and walk about the city. Sometimes he would visit camps of Union soldiers before returning to the White House for breakfast. Benjamin Harrison liked to walk late in the day, after work; sometimes he covered as much as ten miles.

Teddy Roosevelt was yet another president who enjoyed walking. But there was nothing leisurely about Roosevelt's strolls. He called them obstacle walks. He and his fellow hikers would walk in a straight line from their starting point to their destination, without straying even one millimeter from their course. Often their trek would take them up and down the rocky hillsides of Rock Creek Park in northwest Washington. And the party would cross Rock Creek itself, a good-size, fast-moving stream that required each walker to become a swimmer for a few moments. It was considered just as great an honor to be invited on one of Roosevelt's excursions as it was to be asked to play on the White House tennis courts.

In 1908, Roosevelt, in the name of fitness, issued an order

that required all Marine Corps lieutenants and captains to be able to march fifty miles in three days carrying twenty-four pounds of equipment. Early in 1963, when John F. Kennedy was president, General David M. Shoup, commandant of the Marine Corps, discovered the old order and sent it to the president as a historical curiosity.

While President Kennedy's bad back prevented him from doing any serious jogging and put limits on the other physical activities in which he could participate, he had a great interest in sports and physical fitness. In his reply to General Shoup, Kennedy suggested that the general find out "how well our present day officers perform the tests specified by President Roosevelt."

General Shoup ordered a group of marines at Camp Lejeune, North Carolina, to take the test, which they completed within the time limit without any great difficulty. Other marines at other bases accepted the challenge and started hiking. White House staff members and military aides undertook a less rigorous "exhibition hike."

The president's brother, Attorney General Robert F. Kennedy, set out with four friends, rising at dawn in an attempt to complete the trek. His companions dropped out one by one, leaving Kennedy to complete the hike alone.

From one coast to another, people started getting into the act. Boy Scouts took the hike. College students, businessmen, and politicians gave it a try. In Seattle, a group of boys and girls covered the distance on roller skates. In California, 400 high school students set out; ninety-seven of them finished.

A San Francisco newspaper noted: "For good or bad, one of President Kennedy's campaign promises has come true. He's surely got the country moving again."

CHAPTER 2

FITNESS AND FUN

THROUGH THE YEARS, PRESIDENTS IN SEARCH OF FITNESS, fun, or relaxation have turned to almost every type of physical activity and a wide range of recreational pursuits. Benjamin Harrison purchased a rowing machine that could provide a rigorous workout. Rutherford B. Hayes preferred a gentler form of exercise: He installed the first croquet court on the White House grounds. Calvin Coolidge enjoyed daily rides on an electric horse.

When John Quincy Adams became president in 1825, one of the first things he did was install a billiards table in the White House. Adams had learned billiards in Europe during his years of diplomatic service and found the game to be a satisfying form of relaxation.

Adams saw no harm in billing the federal government for the table, balls, and a few cue sticks. As a result, he was immediately denounced as a spendthrift, as a president who squandered the public's money. To put an end to the controversy, Adams paid back the government out of his own funds.

Besides the equipment that presidents have provided for themselves, the Executive Mansion offers an assortment of sports facilities for the use of the first family, aides, and staff members. There's a basement bowling alley and, on the South Grounds, a swimming pool and a tennis court. During George Bush's administration, a putting green, a horseshoe pitching pit, and a basketball hoop and backboard were added.

During recent decades, when aerobics, weight-resistance training, and jogging have gained in popularity, White House residents have frequently pursued these activities. After taking office in 1969, President Richard Nixon sought to have what was termed a "physical conditioning clinic" installed across the street from the White House, in the Old Executive Office Building. When news of the facility leaked out, some members of Congress ripped into the president for spending money foolishly. They called the exercise room a "Roman style romper room . . . really plush."

Presidential press secretary Ron Ziegler rushed to defend what he called "a health unit . . . a very modest facility." He explained that the clinic was meant to replace larger and more elaborate facilities that had been displaced earlier in the year by construction of a new White House press center. The Nixon health facilities included an exercise room with weights, a treadmill, an exercise bicycle, a steam room, a massage table, and a small sunken tile bath equipped with a whirlpool.

"You get here at 6:30 in the morning and you leave at ten at night, and it's good to run a treadmill for ten minutes a day," said Ziegler in defending the installation. President Nixon had not used the new facility, Ziegler said, but had made it available to members of the White House staff.

After Ziegler pointed out that health facilities were available to senators and members of the House of Representatives, that corporations provided gyms for employees, and that similar facilities had existed in at least five other presidential administrations, the controversy died. Nixon must have been thankful he never had to dig into his pocket to pay for the equipment.

During the 1980s, when Ronald Reagan decided he wanted a gym of his own to keep fit, he avoided any wrangling by having the equipment installed in the family quarters on the second floor of the White House. He thus kept the facility off limits to the media and away from the prying eyes of Congress.

Reagan's gym routine began as therapy after he was wounded in an assassination attempt early in 1981. A .22-caliber bullet entered his body under his left arm. Emergency surgery saved his life.

Reagan's White House gym was equipped with an exercycle, a treadmill, and a machine with pulleys and weights that enabled the president to do a variety of exercises for his arms, stomach, shoulders, and legs. The gym also offered an assortment of hand weights, the heaviest of which weighed fifteen pounds. Someone once suggested to Reagan that he get a punching bag. Then whenever he had a rough day, he could paste on the bag a picture of whoever had been tormenting him, and punch away.

After a long day in the Oval Office, Reagan looked forward to working out. His exercise program, designed by a professional, consisted of ten minutes of calisthenics, which was intended to warm up different sets of muscles. This was followed by a fifteen-minute workout on the machines.

Reagan realized that many people have a problem sticking

President Reagan worked out with an exercise machine in the White House. Here he tries out similar equipment at the U.S. Olympic Training Center in Colorado Springs, Colorado. (WIDE WORLD)

to an exercise routine because they get bored. To avoid this, Reagan put some variety into his routines by doing two sets of exercises on alternate days. He also kept the exercise routine as short as possible; it never ran to more than a half an hour. And he also fought off boredom by setting up a TV screen in front of the treadmill. While he walked, Reagan watched the evening news.

Nancy Reagan also used the gym. She did her routine in the morning, using the same equipment her husband used. When the president finished his workout in the evening, he would reset the machines with the lighter weights that she used. He sometimes kiddingly urged her to build up faster so he wouldn't have to keep changing the weights.

Reagan's gym routine produced enormous benefits. Two years after the program began, Reagan had not only fully recovered from the assassination attempt but also, doctors said, was in better shape than when he entered the White House.

George Bush moved into the Executive Mansion following Ronald Reagan's two terms; there's no evidence he got much use out of Reagan's White House gym or the exercise equipment Richard Nixon left behind. Bush was too busy with a long list of other sports.

He enjoyed horseshoes enough to have a horseshoe pit installed next to the White House swimming pool. That was in addition to one at his summer home in Kennebunkport, Maine, and two at Camp David.

The White House pit was built according to official specifications. It consisted of two steel stakes, forty feet apart, surrounded by clay and connected by a narrow concrete walkway. (For women and juniors, the distance between stakes is thirty feet.) When a game was in progress, passersby near the White House could hear the thud of horseshoes landing in the dirt and the clink of one shoe striking another.

There's nothing complicated about horseshoes. Each player has two metal shoes, which are 7½ inches long and weigh 2½ pounds each. The object is to pitch the shoes so that they circle the stake. Each ringer is worth three points. If no ringer is scored, the player whose shoe is nearest the stake earns one point. Games are usually played to twenty-one points.

Bush is said to have discovered horseshoe pitching during the mid-1980s when members of his Secret Service detail, looking for ways to entertain themselves, installed a pit at Bush's Kennebunkport home. Bush happened to see some of the agents enjoying the sport, and joined in. Before long, he was pitching horseshoes at almost every opportunity. He bought two pairs of the U-shaped shoes, and also took out a subscription to *Horseshoe News Digest.*

As this suggests, Bush took the game very seriously. He not only competed against family members, but challenged and defeated members of the press corps, Secret Service agents, and Cabinet members.

With top players, eight out of ten horseshoes end up as ringers. Bush was of average skill, a "25 percenter." Said Donnie Roberts, secretary-treasurer of the National Horseshoe Pitchers Association of America: "That's really good for a guy who picked it up only a few years ago."

In June 1990, when Mikhail Gorbachev, the head of the Soviet Union at the time, was visiting Bush at Camp David, the president invited him to give horseshoes a try. Gorbachev astounded Bush by making a ringer with the first shoe he threw. "Beginner's luck," said veterans of the sport.

George Bush had a horseshoe-pitching pit installed on the South Grounds of the White House. (WIDE WORLD)

Bush wasn't the first president to enjoy horseshoes. He wasn't even the first to install a horseshoe pit on the White House grounds. Credit for that goes to Harry Truman, who frequently invited friends to join him in a game. Herbert Hoover was another horseshoe enthusiast, and so was John Tyler. It is said, in fact, that Tyler, when vice president, was playing a game of horseshoes at his home in Virginia when a messenger rode up with the news that President William Henry Harrison had died.

After Bill Clinton supplanted George Bush in the White House in 1993, he cast the spotlight on bowling, another sport available to White House residents. Clinton was said to be the most enthusiastic bowling president in more than twenty years. As a boy growing up in Hot Springs, Arkansas, Clinton sometimes bowled with friends after school. "It was a casual thing for him, a way to have fun," one of his classmates recalls. "But he was very competitive; he always wanted to win." Clinton took a break from the long federal budget hearings in 1993 to do some bowling.

Bowling made its debut in the White House in 1947, the year Harry Truman was given two lanes by the people of Missouri, his home state. The lanes were installed in the basement of the West Wing. But Dwight Eisenhower, who succeeded Truman, ordered the lanes moved next door to the Old Executive Office Building. That was in 1955. The Eisenhowers weren't interested in bowling and they didn't like hearing the clatter of falling pins.

Bowling made a comeback when Richard Nixon became president in 1959. Nixon himself tried to bowl about once a week, usually late at night. "I bowl seven to twelve games, one after another," he once said. "That gives you a tremen-

Bill Clinton tests his bowling skill during a campaign stop in Lewiston, Maine, early in 1992. (WIDE WORLD)

dous workout." Nixon averaged around 170 and his high game was 232.

"The beauty of bowling," Nixon said, "is that it takes very little time, it's very good for exercise, and it doesn't cost much." Of course, it didn't cost Nixon anything.

The Nixons were a bowling family. The first lady, Patricia Nixon, enjoyed the game, as did the Nixons' daughters, Julie and Tricia.

Since the Nixons found it sometimes inconvenient to walk over to the Old Executive Office Building to bowl, they arranged to have a single bowling lane installed in an underground work space beneath the driveway leading to the North Portico. One enters the lane by walking through the White House kitchen.

During the Clintons' first year in the White House, Chelsea Clinton used the lane when celebrating her thirteenth birthday. Her guests included seventeen friends, most of them from Arkansas. Jimmy Carter's daughter, Amy, who was nine years old when the Carters moved into the White House, also used the lane for bowling parties with her friends.

While Harry Truman was the first president to bowl in the White House, Ulysses S. Grant can be considered the first presidential bowler, according to Bruce Pluckhahn, former curator of the National Bowling Hall of Fame and Museum. On July 4, 1870, the eighteenth president is known to have rolled a bowling ball down a lane that had been installed in a shed behind the Bowen home, known as the "Pink House," in Woodstock, Connecticut. The house and shed are still there.

Abraham Lincoln, as an Illinois congressman, an office he

Richard Nixon, a dedicated bowler, averaged about 170 on the White House lanes. (WIDE WORLD)

held from 1847 to 1849, was "very fond" of bowling, according to Dr. Samuel Busey, who boarded with Lincoln and recorded what he remembered in his *Personal Reminiscences.* Lincoln used the alleys in James Caspari's hotel on Capitol Square, just east of the House of Representatives. This is how Dr. Busey described Lincoln: "He was a very awkward bowler, but played the game with great zest and spirit, solely for exercise and amusement, and greatly to the enjoyment and entertainment of other players and bystanders by his criticisms and funny illustrations. He accepted success and defeat with like nature and humor, and left the alley at the conclusion of the game without a sorrow or disappointment."

Herbert Hoover, the nation's thirty-first president, had a unique method of having fun and trimming his waistline. Hoover relied on medicine ball, a game that resembles volleyball. In medicine ball, a heavy, leather-covered ball, slightly larger than a baseketball and stuffed with soft material, is tossed back and forth over a high net.

Medicine ball was invented just for Hoover, who weighed over 180 pounds when he was elected in November 1928. By the time he was inaugurated, early in March 1929, Hoover's weight had shot up to around 200 pounds because he had attended so many Washington dinner parties.

Naval commander Joel T. Boone, Hoover's personal physician, realized something had to be done and thought up medicine ball. Two teams of two, three, or four players each toss a ten-pound leather ball over a ten-foot-high net. The ball has to be caught on the fly and instantly thrown back. "It required less skill than tennis, was faster and more vigor-

Medicine ball was a favored sport during President Hoover's administration. He and his aides played daily on the South Lawn of the White House. (HERBERT HOOVER PRESIDENTIAL LIBRARY)

ous," Hoover wrote in his *Memoirs*, "and therefore gave more exercise in a short time."

Games were played on the South Lawn at seven o'clock each morning and lasted for about half an hour. Hoover's teammates and opponents included his aides, Cabinet members, Supreme Court justices, and friends. Following the workout, if it wasn't too cold or raining, a light breakfast would sometimes be served outdoors.

Medicine ball lasted until March 4, 1933, the very last day of Hoover's presidency, the day on which Franklin D. Roosevelt was inaugurated. That morning Hoover and other members of what had come to be called the "medicine ball Cabinet" played their final game. Afterward the players said their good-byes and autographed a four-pound souvenir ball, which is now on display at the Herbert Hoover Library in West Branch, Iowa. As far as can be determined, no president before or after Herbert Hoover indulged in medicine ball.

Teddy Roosevelt also participated in a sport for which he alone is known. The sport was single-sticks, a type of fencing in which long, slender lengths of wood were used instead of swords.

The president's opponents were friends who were not afraid of absorbing some physical punishment now and then. Even when one managed to fend off the full force of a rival's stroke, there was always a chance of receiving a glancing blow. "Sometimes we hit hard," Roosevelt said in a letter to a friend, "and today I have a bump over one eye and a swollen wrist."

Roosevelt worked out daily in a gymnasium he had in-

First he chops down a few trees.

Then takes a cross-country canter.

And a twenty-minute brisk walk.

After which he gives the children a wheel-barrow ride.

He then rests for a moment

By which time he is ready for breakfast.

For Teddy Roosevelt, a quiet moment was a rarity. In these cartoons the president is pictured during a vacation stay at Oyster Bay, New York. (LIBRARY OF CONGRESS) stalled in the White House. He wrestled and took jujitsu lessons. He boxed with an assortment of sparring partners, including a former champion. In his quest for fitness, a bump over the eye or a swollen wrist didn't mean much to Teddy Roosevelt.

CHAPTER 3

GOLF:
PRESIDENTIAL CHOICE

I F THERE IS ONE SPORT THAT PRESIDENTS OF THE PAST FIFTY years or so seem to prefer to all others for relaxation, it is golf. Because of lack of space, there is no opportunity to play the game on the White House grounds, but the president can be whisked by limousine to any of several nearby courses whenever he feels the urge to hit the ball and his schedule permits. And family vacations are often planned to provide golfing opportunities.

At one time, presidents used to practice their golf strokes on the South Lawn of the Executive Mansion. But recent presidents who tried that caused crowds of spectators to gather at the fence to watch, and horrendous traffic jams occurred on adjacent streets.

Presidents can now work on their putting, however, on a practice green made of artificial grass that's been installed on the South Grounds just a short chip shot from the swimming pool. Kidney-shaped and with nine holes, the green dates to 1990 and the administration of George Bush, an ardent golfer. Trees and shrubbery shroud the green from the public's view.

A Scottish invention, golf was introduced to the United States during the 1880s. Beginning in the early 1900s, three golfing presidents — William Howard Taft, Woodrow Wilson, and Warren G. Harding — helped to make the sport popular in the United States.

Dwight D. Eisenhower, who occupied the White House from 1953 to 1961, probably played more golf than any other chief executive before or since. And he probably played it more skillfully, too.

Bill Clinton enjoys golf more than any president since Eisenhower. Golf suits his personality: Clinton likes sports that enable him to be friendly and chatty. For Clinton, even jogging is a group activity. Clinton once tried skiing but didn't particularly like it, perhaps because there was no one to talk to on the way down the slope. The same with tennis: There was little chance for conversation. He gave up tennis after he tried golf. When golfing, he can enjoy free and easy banter between partners and opponents.

"He's like a great big jovial host," Roy Neel, a deputy chief of staff and a Clinton golf partner, once said. "His golf game is an extension of him in the sense that he makes people enjoy being with him when he's out there."

Clinton is never in any hurry on the course. A round of golf can last five hours or more. Off the tee, he sees nothing wrong with taking a free shot — called a mulligan — when his previous shot was poorly played. To serious competitors, taking a mulligan is something like getting four strikes in baseball.

Clinton not only takes extra shots himself, he encourages others to do so. During a 1993 family vacation on Martha's

President Clinton watches his ball after teeing off on a course in Rogers, Arkansas, in 1993. (WIDE WORLD)

Vineyard, an island off Cape Cod, Clinton played golf with Vernon Jordan, a well-known Washington lawyer. After Jordan pushed his tee shot behind a tree, Clinton urged him to take another. "You've got to get a good shot on the first tee, Vernon," Clinton said. Clinton's friends did not feel the

President Clinton reacts without joy as he checks his scorecard during a golf match on Martha's Vineyard. The Clintons vacationed there in 1993. (WIDE WORLD)

president was breaking the rules, but only showing a generosity of spirit.

For somebody who doesn't get out on the course very often, Clinton plays well, shooting in the high 80s or low 90s (not counting the mulligans). He has a fluid swing and can boom the ball a long distance off the tee, but it often veers to the left or right and into trouble. "He doesn't know where the ball is going," a friend once said, "but he loves the game."

While Bill Clinton is calm and relaxed on the golf course,

President Bush liked to zip around the golf course; he played speed golf.
(NATIONAL ARCHIVES)

George Bush, Clinton's predecessor in the White House, was anything but. On family vacations in Kennebunkport, Bush often played golf at the Cape Arundel Golf Club, where his father once held the course record. The president liked to whiz around the course, hurrying almost every shot, driving his cart at breakneck speed between holes. Bush's goal was to finish eighteen holes in the shortest time possible. Speed golf, it was called.

"He plays twice as fast as the normal player," said Ken Raynor, the golf professional at Cape Arundel and a friend of Bush's, who often played with him. Bush once finished eighteen holes in one hour and twenty-five minutes, his personal record. The average player requires over four hours.

"Golf clears the mind," Bush once told an interviewer from *Sports Illustrated*. "I don't concentrate too much out there. I'm in it for the competition."

Bush usually shot in the 80s, a respectable score for an occasional golfer. He was good off the tee, often driving the ball about 250 yards. "He's got that old baseball swing," Raynor once noted.

Bush's biggest problem was putting. After he had lined up the ball and was getting ready to strike it, he often experienced a nervous spasm, which golfers call the yips. Raynor said, "He'd rather face Congress than a three-foot putt."

In an effort to rid himself of the yips, Bush tried many different putters and putting styles. He even tried putting one-handed. Nothing seemed to work. Finally, Ken Raynor gave him a putter with an exceptionally long shaft, fifty-two inches. The long club made Bush stand erect over the golf ball, allowing him to line it up better, and his putting improved.

But what really helped the president's score more than the long-handled putter or the constant stream of advice he got from Ken Raynor—or anyone else—were the "gimmes" he received. His friendly opponents seldom made him putt any ball that was less than seven or eight feet from the hole. Sometimes Bush would ask for an opponent to concede a putt, saying, "Out of respect for the high office of the presi-

Putting was a never-ending problem for President Bush. (WIDE WORLD)

dency, isn't that putt good?" Bush opponents would invariably say yes.

Gerald R. Ford, one of the most athletic presidents, enjoyed a wide variety of sports, golf among them. He starred in football at the University of Michigan and also developed boxing and wrestling skills. While earning a law degree at

President Ford practices at Camp David in 1975. Aspen Lodge is in the background. (GERALD R. FORD LIBRARY)

Yale, Ford was assistant football and boxing coach. During his presidential term, which began in 1974 upon the resignation of President Richard Nixon, Ford enjoyed swimming, jogging, and skiing, as well as golf. Like Bill Clinton, Ford usually scored in the high 80s or low 90s.

Ford liked to play in celebrity golf tournaments. In these, he would be teamed up with a top professional. Claiming that none of the pros with whom he was teamed ever won the tournament, Ford called himself the "jinx of the links."

The bad luck Ford visited upon his golfing partners occasionally extended to his own game. Several times, Ford hit golf balls that struck spectators. This caused comedian Bob Hope, a frequent partner of presidents, to joke: "You never have to count his score, just count the casualties."

Lyndon B. Johnson and Richard Nixon also liked golf, but played only occasionally. Nixon wanted no interference when he played. He once wrote a memo to his chief of staff, H. R. Haldeman, explaining how he felt. "When clubs allow photographers," Nixon said, "I will not play."

Golf was a sport John F. Kennedy enjoyed. The second-oldest of four boys, Kennedy tried his best in such sports as football, baseball, and swimming in prep school, but never managed to win a letter in any of them. He played softball and hockey in an intramural league. "I wasn't a good athlete," he once said, "but I participated."

Later, at Harvard University, he went out for football. When he failed to make the varsity team, he was assigned to the junior varsity. During a scrimmage, Kennedy hurt his back; the injury caused him pain through most of the rest of his life.

Despite his bad back, Kennedy continued to play golf. He had a no-nonsense style. "Jack never fusses," said Bert Nicolls, a Palm Beach, Florida, golf professional. "He just walks up and hits the ball." Kennedy often shot in the 70s, a score that indicates he might have become the best of the golfing presidents.

Kennedy reinjured his back at a tree-planting ceremony in Ottawa, Canada, in May 1961. Doctors told him he could no longer play golf. But he did play on at least one other occasion. In the summer of 1963, he and Mrs. Kennedy played a few holes together near the family compound at Hyannisport on Nantucket Sound. In November of that year, Kennedy was assassinated.

Golf was the favorite sport of Dwight D. Eisenhower, another athletic president. From Abilene, Kansas, Eisenhower was a star in baseball and football in high school. Later, at the U.S. Military Academy at West Point, he made a name for himself not only in baseball and football but in boxing and track as well. Eisenhower was also a devoted fly fisherman and a marksman with both pistol and shotgun. But when Eisenhower was president, golf was his number one sport.

Although Eisenhower tried golf at an early age, he didn't take up the game seriously until he was in his fifties. He worked hard to become skilled. He took lessons; he practiced almost without letup. Anytime he blundered on the course, he would keep practicing the shot until he got it right. He rejoiced when he played well, but when he unleashed one of his wild slices or his score zoomed into the 90s, his mood would darken.

During the years of his presidency, Eisenhower's critics constantly claimed he spent too much time golfing. His physician, Major General Howard Snyder, defended him. "Golf is a tonic for the president," he said. "It's good for his nerves and muscle tone, and it takes his mind off of the anxieties that confront him daily. I say he should play whenever he gets a chance."

Eisenhower didn't disagree with this advice. He usually played on Wednesdays and Saturdays at Burning Tree Country Club near Washington.

Soon after Eisenhower became the thirty-fourth presi-

Golf was Dwight D. Eisenhower's number one sport during his presidency. (DWIGHT D. EISENHOWER LIBRARY)

dent, a practice facility was built for him at Camp David. Installed in a clearing below the spacious lodge where the president and his family stayed, it took the form of a slightly elevated green that could be approached from four directions, each at a different distance and level. Eisenhower practiced his chipping and putting there by the hour.

Eisenhower sought to improve his game at every opportunity. He had not occupied the White House for very long before passersby began to see him practicing chipping on the South Lawn. Once his routine became well known, spectators would gather at the fence to watch. Motorists even left their cars on nearby streets to run up to the fence and take a look. Honking horns and cursing drivers resulted.

Despite the traffic jams, Eisenhower gave no thought to abandoning the sessions, but he did seek to outwit the onlookers. Whenever he was practicing and a crowd began to assemble, Eisenhower would duck into a police sentry booth and wait there until the gawkers left. Then he'd resume practicing.

In 1954, the U.S. Golf Association installed a putting green in a tree-shrouded area just outside the Oval Office, where Eisenhower could practice unseen by the public. To one side of the green, a small sand trap was installed.

Since trees and bushes concealed the green from the street, the public was no longer a problem. But squirrels were. Families of squirrels who lived on the White House grounds looked upon the new green as an ideal storage area for their acorns and began digging holes in it. When Eisenhower complained that his green was being ravaged, staff members ordered the squirrels to be trapped, then removed from the Executive Mansion's grounds and released in some distant park. Local newspapers got wind of the story and a

President Eisenhower worked hard to improve his game. Here he practices at Camp David. (DWIGHT D. EISENHOWER LIBRARY)

storm of controversy broke. A "Save the Squirrels Fund" was organized, with the goal of protecting the White House's bushy-tailed rodents. All trapping and removal operations were immediately halted.

Eventually, the story faded from the headlines and Eisenhower was able to putt in peace again, even if the green was a little bit bumpy. During his White House years, he got plenty of use out of it. Since it was right outside his office door, Eisenhower was able to duck out and start stroking whenever there was a lull in the day's activities. After Richard Nixon became president in 1969, he had the putting green removed.

Eisenhower left office in 1961, to be succeeded by John F. Kennedy. Magazine writer John Devaney visited the Oval Office that year to interview a Kennedy aide. Devaney noticed that the office carpet still displayed countless small punctures made by Eisenhower's golf cleats.

In 1909, when William Howard Taft became president, golf was looked upon as a sport for rich, white, middle-aged men. It was played at a handful of exclusive country clubs in the East, and almost nowhere else in the United States. The world's best players came from England and Scotland, and they won virtually all of the major tournaments.

William Howard Taft, the twenty-seventh president, helped to change all that. The largest of America's chief executives, Taft was almost six feet tall and weighed more than 300 pounds. Despite his size, Taft pioneered presidential interest in a number of sports.

He was the first president to take up golf seriously. Teddy Roosevelt, the president who preceded Taft, rejected the game because he thought it to be "undemocratic" and "too much of a sissy's game." Roosevelt is said to have wondered how any man could ever play it.

Taft, on the other hand, loved the game and made no secret of the fact. "It's a game for people who are not active enough for baseball or tennis," he once said, "or who have too much weight to carry around to play those games; and yet when a man weighs 295 pounds you have to give him some opportunity to make his legs and insides move, and golf offers that."

During his White House term, Taft played golf two or three times a week. Although he had an unusual short, choppy swing, he often scored in the 90s, and sometimes in the 80s. He once described his game as "bumble-puppy" golf.

Woodrow Wilson, who defeated both Taft and Teddy Roosevelt in the election of 1912, also liked golf for its fitness benefits. Wilson's scores were usually well above 100, but he didn't care. He just seemed to enjoy whacking the ball from one hole to the next, never minding much where it happened to land.

Wilson tried to play every day. He would usually leave the White House promptly at 8:30 A.M., arrive at the golf course within fifteen minutes, spend a couple of hours batting the ball around, and be back in the White House, showered, dressed, and ready to begin his workday, at eleven o'clock.

Wilson even played during the winter months, bundling up in a warm sweater and cap. Even snow didn't stop him: He had the balls painted red so they could be more easily spotted against the snow-covered ground.

Wilson wanted no distractions when he played, nor did he

William Howard Taft was the first of the golfing presidents. (LIBRARY OF CONGRESS)

want to be reminded of the burdens of his office. His most frequent golfing companion was Dr. Cary T. Grayson, his physician. Dr. Grayson once explained that the president preferred his company because "most men whom he invited to play with him insisted on introducing public business into the conversation."

The day after the 1916 election, won by Wilson, he was playing golf with Dr. Grayson, when the pair encountered other players near the final hole. "How is your game today?" one of them called out. The president waved a greeting and smiled. "The doctor has me by three strokes," he said. "But I don't care. I'm four states ahead in yesterday's election."

Four years later, Warren G. Harding succeeded Wilson to become the third consecutive golfing president. But unlike Wilson and Taft, Harding worked hard to improve his game and reduce his score.

Harding was serious-minded when it came to golf. He wanted no "mulligans" or "gimmes." He stuck by the rules. On one occasion, when golfing friends told him to pick up a ball that looked to be unplayable and move it, Harding refused. "Forget that I'm the president of the United States," he said. "I'm Warren Harding playing with some friends, and I'm going to beat the hell out of them."

Once a match got under way, Harding would stride down the fairways at a rapid pace, eager to get to his ball and execute the next shot. Sometimes his golfing companions had trouble keeping up with him. Once, playing with Ring Lardner, a noted short-story writer and humorist, Harding left the tee even before Lardner had taken his drive. After marching down the fairway for a hundred or so yards, Harding stood aside and watched Lardner swing. Lardner sliced the ball, which struck high in a tree near where the president was standing. A small branch fell down and hit Harding on the shoulder. Lardner, walking up to the president, pretended not to be concerned. Grinning, he said: "I was just trying to make Coolidge president." (Calvin Coolidge was Harding's vice president.) Harding laughed heartily.

Harding's golf scores were not made public. But his secretary once revealed that the president was "tickled to death" anytime he shot in the low 90s. Although he was very serious about the game, he joked with his golfing companions during a round and often took along Laddie Boy, his pet Scottie. Harding always wore knickers, the fashion of the time, when he played.

Harding died in office in 1923. He was succeeded by Calvin Coolidge, who, at the time he moved into the Executive Mansion, had virtually no interest in sports. There would be no golf-playing president for three decades, until Dwight D. Eisenhower and his clubs moved into the Executive Mansion in 1953.

CHAPTER 4

ON THE COURT

AMERICAN PRESIDENTS ARE ABLE TO PLAY TENNIS ON what could well be the most exclusive court on earth. It's a hard court with a slight give to it that's nestled amidst thick shrubbery and leafy trees on the South Grounds of the White House. Presidents and their families play there, as do presidential aides and Cabinet members. For anyone else, a special invitation is required, and such invitations are rarely issued.

Tourists used to be able to peek through the tall iron fence that encloses the White House grounds and catch a glimpse of the players. But during the Kennedy administration, Mrs. Kennedy had White House gardeners plant a screen of magnolia trees and holly bushes to conceal the court and its players.

During the summer, wrought-iron tables, shaded by big umbrellas, are set out. Plantings of white azaleas and red geraniums help beautify the site. There's a refrigerator stocked with sodas, and a telephone to keep the president, his partner, and their opponents linked to the outside world.

President Ford gets set to unleash a forehand stroke. (GERALD R. FORD LIBRARY)

While Bill Clinton rarely uses the court, George Bush played frequently, as did Jimmy Carter and Gerald Ford. Carter, in fact, liked to keep track of when White House staff members were using the court. Critics cited this as an example of how he had allowed himself to get bogged down in the unimportant details of his job.

George Bush began playing tennis when he was about five years old. His mother gave him lessons. "She was a good tennis player," Bush once told *Tennis* magazine, "a real scrapper, a tough competitor."

Besides teaching young George the basic strokes, she also schooled him in court manners, attempting to check his tendency to boast. Once, following a defeat, young George claimed to have been "off my game." His mother jumped all over him. "You don't even *have* a game," she told him.

Tennis was one of several sports enjoyed by Jimmy Carter. Here the president is pictured with Hamilton Jordan, an aide. (JIMMY CARTER LIBRARY)

Although President Bush was a natural left-hander—he signed his name, threw a baseball, and stirred his morning coffee with his left hand—he played tennis right-handed.

An avid tennis player, President Bush used the White House tennis court frequently. (NATIONAL ARCHIVES)

This trait he traced back to when he was a child of five or six and beginning to learn tennis, and his mother made him hold the racket in his right hand. "In those days," as Bush once explained, "you weren't allowed to be left-handed."

As president, Bush played on the White House court about twice a week during warm months. He always played doubles, the version of the game with two players to a side. His ground strokes were, according to his own estimation, "terrible," but he made up for this failing by being an aggressive player who liked to race to the net and slam the ball hard for a winner.

It was said that Bush sized up people by the way they played the game. Marlin Fitzwater, Bush's press secretary, once noted, "Subconsciously, at least, the president judges people by their competitive attitude on the court. He likes people who are competitive as well as fun."

Bush himself said: "I'm a great believer that sports can do wonders for friendships and establishing common ground. Have always felt that way."

Bush became friends with James A. Baker when the pair teamed up to win the doubles championship at the Houston Country Club in the late 1950s. When Bush became president, he named Baker to be his secretary of state.

Bush met Nicholas Brady, who became a close friend, on a tennis court. Brady served as secretary of the treasury in the Bush administration.

His friends and advisers knew that Bush considered tennis to be a very serious matter and seldom, if ever, talked business on the court. But once, when pressed for time, Roger Porter, Bush's domestic policy chief, mentioned something to the president on the court. Porter recalled, "Afterward, everyone said, 'How did you get to him so fast?'"

President Ford (left) and George Bush, long before his presidency began, team up in a doubles match. (GERALD R. FORD LIBRARY)

When others were using the court, Bush would occasionally leave the Oval Office, and with Millie, the first family's dog, stroll down to the court to watch a few games. He liked to keep track of who was playing well — and who wasn't — so teams could later be arranged that would provide close competition.

One of George Bush's idols, Teddy Roosevelt, got tennis started at the White House. In 1902, Roosevelt ordered a rolled-dirt court installed just outside the executive offices. He could step from his office right out onto the court.

When Roosevelt was criticized for what was described as needless expenditure, he argued that the $400 it cost him to have the court built was far less than what Presidents Ulysses S. Grant, Benjamin Harrison, and Grover Cleveland each had spent on White House greenhouses.

Roosevelt also pointed out that the court was going to be used by his children, four boys and two girls. "It surely cannot be meant that there is any objection to the president and his children playing tennis," wrote Roosevelt at the time, "and of course it is impossible for them to play tennis except on the White House grounds."

While he may have intended the court for the use of his children, it was Roosevelt himself who used it the most. Even on summer afternoons when the soaring temperature and humidity made it difficult to get a breath of air, Roosevelt and his aides would be caught up in tense games. Sometimes diplomats and political leaders were made to wait outside his office while Roosevelt finished a hotly contested match.

Roosevelt liked tennis because it offered plenty of excitement and nonstop action. But he played the game in an unusual way. He gripped the racket halfway up the handle, with his index finger pressing hard against the shaft, which gave him a short but powerful swing. While he could hit the ball hard, Roosevelt's special joy was to angle a return into a distant corner, beyond his opponent's reach.

Like George Bush, Roosevelt played for keeps. Once during a match, Archie Butt, a Roosevelt adviser and frequent player, slammed a ball at the president and struck him in the head. Butt rushed toward the net to apologize, but Roosevelt

Father plays tennis with Mr. Cooley. ———

In a picture letter to his children, President Theodore Roosevelt drew this cartoon of a tennis match between himself (on the left) and a Mr. Cooley. (NEW YORK PUBLIC LIBRARY)

waved him away. "If I hit you, *I'm* not going to apologize," Roosevelt said, "so just bang away at me as much as you like and say nothing in the fray."

While tennis matches during Roosevelt's administration included a wide range of the president's friends and political acquaintances, he usually drew his partners from a group of young government officials. Some of these became Roosevelt's close personal friends and trusted advisers. Newspapers of the time sometimes referred to this group as Roosevelt's Tennis Cabinet. Playing tennis with the president could help to guarantee a bright political future, it was said.

After Roosevelt left office in 1909 to be succeeded by William Howard Taft, an avid golfer, the tennis court was torn up to build the Oval Office. This distressed Helen Taft, the president's wife, who realized that tennis had social value. A White House court would be a good place for her three teenagers to entertain their friends. At Mrs. Taft's urging, another court was built on the southwest side of the South Grounds, which is the site of the present court.

The White House court was touched by tragedy in 1924 during Calvin Coolidge's first administration. On June 30 of that year, the Coolidges' two sons, Calvin and John, played a match that left sixteen-year-old Calvin with a blister on the big toe of his right foot. The blister became infected, and seven days later young Calvin died of blood poisoning. (Penicillin, which would almost certainly have saved his life, was not developed until 1941.)

The court has also served as a setting for festive times. When Richard and Pat Nixon's daughter Tricia got married in 1971, newspaper and television reporters were welcomed and entertained under a huge tent erected over the court.

During the Reagan administration, the White House tennis court was the site of Nancy Reagan's annual party to raise money for her antidrug charity. Professional tennis stars and celebrities were the featured guests.

Ronald Reagan much preferred horseback riding to tennis. "I used to play when I was young," he once said with a grin, "but I don't anymore because I can't get the horse on the court."

CHAPTER 5

IN
SWIMMING

MANY PRESIDENTS WERE EXCELLENT SWIMMERS. Some swam for health and strength. To others, swimming was just plain fun. But to Ronald Reagan, the forty-first president, swimming was serious business. He is the only president who achieved the status of hero as a swimmer.

During his high school years, Reagan worked as a lifeguard at a recreation area on the Rock River near the small town of Dixon, Illinois, where his family lived. Reagan is said to have put a notch in a log each time he saved a person from drowning. In his six summers as a lifeguard, Reagan made seventy-one notches.

As president, Reagan liked the pool at Camp David better than the White House pool because it offered greater privacy. But when he had a choice, Reagan much preferred the ocean. Swimming in the surf, he said, provided vigorous exercise without the monotony of swimming laps.

Reagan once admitted that he liked to show off for his wife, Nancy, by doing such fancy dives as the jackknife

After working as a lifeguard during his high school years, Reagan joined the swimming team at Eureka College. (EUREKA COLLEGE)

and swan dive. "I guess it's the old lifeguard in me," he joked.

"My old specialty, the backjack, is still in decent enough shape to teach kids how to do it," Reagan once told *Parade* magazine. "You stand with your back to the water, toes near

President Reagan, with Mrs. Reagan at his side, splashes water on himself as he prepares to take a swim at Kahala Beach in Hawaii in 1984. (WIDE WORLD)

the end of the board, push off backwards, then touch your toes and straighten out before you enter the water.

"It makes Nancy nervous," Reagan added, "and gives jitters to my agents, but kids love it."

Recent presidents, such as Ronald Reagan, have been able to swim without leaving home, because the White House now has its own swimming pool. It dates to 1975 and the administration of Gerry Ford. Presidents of an earlier day saw no need for a pool to enjoy swimming. For example, John Quincy Adams, the sixth president, would rise between four and five o'clock in the morning, then walk for several miles or mount one of the horses from the White House stable and ride. When the day was warm, Adams liked to slip down to the Potomac River, about a mile from the White House, for a swim. After he had undressed, Adams would fold his clothes and leave them on the riverbank. Early risers could spot the president frolicking in midriver. After his swim, Adams would dress, then return to the White House to read his Bible and the morning newspaper before breakfast at nine o'clock.

Presidents Zachary Taylor, Ulysses S. Grant, and William McKinley were also skilled swimmers. But not until 1901, when Teddy Roosevelt took up residence in the White House, did any president again take off his clothes to test the waters of the Potomac.

Roosevelt would sometimes lead groups of friends on hiking expeditions that began at the White House. These jaunts would often end up at the Potomac River or Rock Creek, several miles from the White House. A swim followed. "If we swam in the Potomac," Roosevelt once recalled, "we took off our clothes." But it was not unusual for Roosevelt to plunge into the water fully clothed. "What difference does it make?" he asked. "It was the shortest, quickest way, and a wetting does no harm."

Franklin D. Roosevelt, the thirty-second president and a distant cousin of Teddy Roosevelt's, was the first chief executive to enjoy the convenience of a White House pool. Roosevelt moved into the Executive Mansion in 1933.

Growing up, Roosevelt had only a mild interest in sports and recreational activities, although he had an athletic build, standing six feet, two inches and weighing 170 pounds. He tried out for freshman football in college but failed to make the team. He rode horseback and played some golf. If there was any sport that excited him, it was sailing. He learned to sail the waters around the family's summer home on Campobello, a sparsely populated island between the coasts of Maine and Canada's New Brunswick.

During August 1921, while he was vacationing with his wife and children at Campobello, Roosevelt, then thirty-nine, was touched by tragedy. He fell suddenly ill and developed a high fever. The next morning, he experienced intense pain in his legs.

Roosevelt had suffered an attack of poliomyelitis, also called polio, a disease that often leaves its victims paralyzed for life. In Roosevelt's time and before, epidemics of polio, which often struck infants and young children, were not uncommon. A vaccine that became the first effective weapon in preventing polio was not developed until the 1950s.

After the polio attack, Roosevelt was never able to use his legs. To stand, he needed crutches or heavy leg braces. Most of his waking hours were spent in a wheelchair.

The only time Roosevelt could experience any freedom of movement was when his lower body was submerged in water. Roosevelt began to visit a health resort at Warm Springs, Georgia, to use the huge swimming pool there. The pool had a constant temperature of eighty-eight degrees and was fed by an underground spring rich in cal-

To Franklin Roosevelt, Warm Springs was a place where he could relax and in whose heated waters he could enjoy freedom of movement. (FRANKLIN D. ROOSEVELT LIBRARY)

At Warm Springs, Roosevelt enjoyed splashing alongside other polio victims, children as well as adults. (FRANKLIN D. ROOSEVELT LIBRARY)

cium and magnesium. Roosevelt spent countless hours in the pool performing leg exercises under a doctor's supervision.

"Every morning I spend two hours in the most wonderful pool in the world," Roosevelt wrote to a friend, "and it is no exaggeration to say that the muscles in my legs have improved to an extent noticeable in every way." Although Roo-

President Roosevelt and his wife Eleanor take a swimming break at the pool at the family home in Hyde Park, New York. (FRANKLIN D. ROOSEVELT LIBRARY)

sevelt was optimistic about his chances for recovery, doctors knew he would never get back the use of his legs.

Roosevelt invested his own money to improve and expand the facilities at Warm Springs. As the health resort became better known, polio sufferers from every part of the country began to visit it. After Roosevelt became president, a "Birthday Ball" was held each January to raise money for Warm Springs and for polio prevention.

To Roosevelt, Warm Springs was a place where he could

relax and close his mind to the burdens of the office. It made him happy to be able to splash alongside other polio sufferers, children as well as adults.

Not long after Roosevelt became president in 1933, the New York *Daily News* launched a fund-raising drive to construct a White House swimming pool. A dozen other papers joined in the effort, asking the public for contributions, which poured in. Children donated their pennies. Within a short time, enough money had been raised to build a splendid pool and dressing rooms.

Roosevelt used the pool almost every evening, quitting work around 5:30 for an hour's swim before dinner. While he could not use his paralyzed legs, his arm, shoulder, and back muscles were so well developed that he could outswim every member of his staff.

Late in March 1945, a worn and tired Roosevelt made his final journey to Warm Springs. It was there, on April 12, 1945, that he suffered the stroke that took his life.

Within ten years of Roosevelt's death, Dr. Jonas Salk developed the vaccine now used to immunize children against the polio virus.

Harry Truman, who became president upon Roosevelt's death, referred to the White House pool as his "swimming hole." However, neither he nor Dwight D. Eisenhower shared Roosevelt's passion for swimming. But toward the end of his first term, Eisenhower suffered a heart attack. As part of his recovery program, Eisenhower's doctors persuaded him to swim for thirty minutes around noontime each day.

John Kennedy was another president who reaped health benefits from the White House swimming pool. He often swam before lunch and again in the early evening. The

At Harvard, John F. Kennedy (back row, third from left) was a dedicated member of the swimming team. (WIDE WORLD)

workouts helped ease the back pain that Kennedy often endured.

Kennedy was an outstanding swimmer. At Harvard, he was a dedicated and enthusiastic member of the swimming team. "Have been in strict training for a month now and get off tomorrow night as we swim against Yale," Kennedy wrote to a friend at Princeton. "Have taken eight seconds off my time and am now down to 107 [one minute, seven seconds] in the 100 [100-yard freestyle]."

Once, just before an important meet, Kennedy came down with the flu and was placed in the college infirmary for treat-

Relaxing in the White House pool, President Lyndon Johnson (right) confers with two aides. (LYNDON BAINES JOHNSON LIBRARY)

ment. Afraid that he wouldn't be strong enough to compete, he had a friend smuggle milk shakes and steaks into his infirmary room. And from time to time, he would rush out to the practice pool, swim a few laps, and then hurry back to his bed before his absence could be discovered.

Lyndon Johnson, Kennedy's vice president, who became president following Kennedy's assassination, also enjoyed

President Johnson enjoys a swim at the LBJ Ranch with Mrs. Johnson
and the family's pet beagle. (LYNDON BAINES JOHNSON LIBRARY)

the White House pool, often swimming with his aides. Johnson also had a big outdoor pool at the LBJ Ranch. That pool
could be heated, which enabled the president and his friends
to take dips in cold weather.

When Richard Nixon became president, he supervised
several alterations to the White House, one of which served
to do away with the swimming pool. Nixon converted a
press lobby in the West Wing into a reception area. Then, to
accommodate the press, he had the swimming pool covered
over and a press room built on top.

Nixon was forced to resign in 1974 in the aftermath of
the Watergate scandal, and Gerald Ford became president.
Ford immediately began to campaign for the construction
of an outdoor swimming pool. It took several weeks to

President Gerald Ford tests the waters of the White House swimming pool during dedication ceremonies in 1975. (GERALD R. FORD LIBRARY)

decide upon the location, which is about sixty feet south of the West Wing, where Ford had his office. The site was occupied by air-conditioned dog kennels built by President Johnson. The Fords had no interest in dogs; their only pet was a cat.

Completed in 1975, the pool is long and narrow, 54.8 feet long and 22 feet wide. It is 3 feet deep at the shallow end and 9 feet at the deep end, with a 10-foot diving board. There's a small cabana nearby. But the old White House pool, built for Franklin D. Roosevelt and used frequently by Dwight Eisenhower, Jack Kennedy, and Lyndon Johnson, is still there—empty of water, of course, and covered over by the press room.

CHAPTER 6

WITH ROD AND REEL

IT LEVELS PEOPLE OUT," JIMMY CARTER ONCE TOLD EDItor and author Howell Raines. "The trout don't care if you're President of the United States or a local farmer or a high school kid."

That was one of the several values Carter saw in fly-fishing, a sport to which he was deeply devoted. He also enjoyed its constant challenge. He said it required "a kind of stalking" and "a great element of patience." Fly fishermen, Carter told Raines, "really spend a lot of time observing a pool or a stream or current before they ever put a fly in the water."

Among the presidents who were anglers and shared Carter's feelings about fishing were George Bush, Dwight D. Eisenhower, Herbert Hoover, and Grover Cleveland. Not all, however, were dedicated fly fishermen, as Carter was, skilled at catching fish with slim and supple rods and artificial insects fashioned from feathers and thread. Still other presidents were mere bait fishermen, whose joy came from simply catching fish. They didn't care too much about technique.

President Jimmy Carter was an ardent fly fisherman. The sport "levels people out," he said. (JIMMY CARTER LIBRARY)

During the early 1990s, fly-fishing enjoyed a period of remarkable growth, which was due in part to the popularity of Robert Redford's movie *A River Runs Through It.* Fly-fishing enthusiasts saw the sport as a way to "get back to nature." Hunting satisfied that urge, too, except that people were becoming more and more uneasy about the use of guns.

As president, Jimmy Carter fished in Big Hunting Creek at Camp David and in ponds near his hometown of Plains,

Georgia. Carter also tied his own flies. In 1991, the museum of the Jimmy Carter Library in Atlanta featured an exhibition, "The Tie That Binds," concerning Carter's hobby. Carter's special fly-tying desk was included in the exhibit.

George Bush was another enthusiastic fisherman. At one time or another, Bush fished for bluefish, bass, bonefish, white marlin, tarpon, and sailfish. Bluefish, native to the Atlantic coast, were his favorite. "I don't like the big stuff as much," he said.

When vacationing in Kennebunkport, Bush would take his twenty-eight-foot racing boat, *Fidelity*, and try to get to where the bluefish were. He loved maneuvering the boat through rocky inlets and hidden coves and racing across stretches of open ocean with the throttle wide open. The Secret Service agents were forced to increase the speed of their chase boat, because more than once Bush took off without warning, leaving them behind in his wake.

The bluefish Bush caught averaged about ten pounds, but he once got a seventeen-pounder off Boon Island, about twenty or so miles down the coast from Kennebunkport. Most of the blues Bush and his companions caught were released.

On most fishing excursions aboard *Fidelity*, Bush was accompanied by one or more of his sons and other family members. *Fidelity* could accommodate six or seven people. Bob Boilard, a retired navy employee and a neighbor of Bush's, was another of his favorite companions. "It's a shame that he can't spend more time on the water," Boilard once told *Sports Illustrated*. "When he's got a rod in one hand, the steering wheel in the other and everything under control, there's not a happier man anywhere."

Bush also enjoyed bonefishing off Islamorada, halfway

President Bush tries fly casting in the Kennebunk River in Kennebunkport, Maine. (WIDE WORLD)

Fishing excursions gave Bush the chance to zip along in his twenty-eight-foot racing boat. (NATIONAL ARCHIVES)

down the Florida Keys, the chain of islands that stretches southeast from Miami. The bonefish is one of the world's great game fish. With silvery scales and a skeleton made up of small, fine bones, the bonefish has an average weight of around six pounds, but anyone who has ever hooked into one knows the bonefish feels like a sixty-pounder once it starts to fight.

Along with George Hommell, Jr.—a Florida fishing guide—and a Secret Service agent, Bush would set out at around daybreak in a seventeen-foot skiff powered by a 110-horsepower outboard engine. Often the trio spent seven or eight hours on the water.

Bush had the first bonefish he ever caught mounted. All the others he released. (Because of all those tiny bones, the bonefish is not good to eat.)

Bush often spoke of how fishing gave him time to relax

and think. "He really loves it out there," Hommell said in an article in *Sports Illustrated*.

Dwight D. Eisenhower, like Jimmy Carter, was a fly fisherman who liked to tie his own flies. He used a bamboo rod—a relic of the past—and a reel that had to be hand wound. "I used a bamboo rod when I started fishing as a kid," Ike once said, "and I just got used to it. I prefer the old-fashioned reel because I like to play my fish—wind the line myself. As for the dry fly, I feel it's a more natural way to fish for trout."

Once, at a meeting of the Eisenhower Cabinet, Vice President Richard Nixon and Oveta Culp Hobby, secretary of health, education, and welfare, presented the president with an assortment of flies on behalf of the Cabinet. Tickled pink at the gift, Eisenhower couldn't wait to try out the flies. He tied one to a line and made a gentle cast in the Cabinet room. The hook caught press secretary Jim Hagerty by the seat of the trousers, and no one could get it free. Eisenhower eventually had to cut the line with a pocketknife, leaving Hagerty to walk off with the fly.

Eisenhower fished in many parts of the country—in Maine, South Dakota, Maryland, Georgia, and Wisconsin. He once invited former president Hoover to join him on a fishing expedition in Colorado. When newspaper reporters swarmed around the two men, Hoover got upset. He said, "I used to believe there were only two occasions in which the American people had regard for the privacy of the president—in prayer and in fishing. I now detect you have lost the second part."

Harry Truman, who fished the Missouri River when he was a boy growing up in Independence, Missouri, was not an enthusiastic fisherman during his years as president, but

President Eisenhower tries his hand at trout fishing during a visit to Custer State Park in South Dakota. (DWIGHT D. EISENHOWER LIBRARY)

President Truman during a fishing trip off Hamilton, Bermuda, in 1946. (WIDE WORLD)

he occasionally went deep-sea fishing in the waters off Key West, Florida, where the Trumans vacationed.

Franklin D. Roosevelt enjoyed ocean fishing, too. It was, in fact, one of his favorite leisure activities. Although polio had paralyzed his legs, Roosevelt had unusually strong arms and shoulders, which enabled him to be extremely proficient as a deep-sea angler. He once caught a 230-pound shark after a battle that lasted an hour and a half.

Another time, Roosevelt hooked a sailfish off the Cocos Islands in the Indian Ocean. He was struggling with it when a second sailfish hit his line. The first sailfish escaped, but the second one's spearlike beak was entangled, and Roosevelt managed to get the fish into the boat. After having it mounted, Roosevelt displayed the sailfish at the White House, with his line still snarled about its beak.

During the summer of 1941, Roosevelt told the press he was going fishing aboard the presidential yacht off Martha's Vineyard. But he really didn't have fishing in mind. Following his departure from Washington, Roosevelt sent daily messages to newspaper reporters, saying the weather was fine and the fishing good. Several days went by before the true reason for the expedition was revealed. The presidential yacht had actually cruised all the way north to Placentia Bay off Newfoundland. There Roosevelt secretly met British prime minister Winston Churchill. On August 14, 1941, the two men signed the Atlantic Charter. World War II was raging in Europe and parts of Asia at the time, and the charter's declaration of principles expressed objectives to be sought in the postwar world.

Like Roosevelt, Herbert Hoover used fishing as a way to escape the pressure of the presidency. And during Hoover's term, there was plenty of pressure. Less than a year after he

What was announced as a fishing trip for President Roosevelt (left) during the summer of 1941 ended in a conference with Great Britain's prime minister, Winston Churchill (right), and the signing of the Atlantic Charter. (WIDE WORLD)

was elected in 1928, the stock market crashed, launching the Great Depression. Industrial plants shut their doors, throwing millions out of work. Thousands of banks failed. Hoover's popularity nosedived. Once, when he attended a baseball game, the crowd booed him.

Even before his inauguration in 1929, Hoover knew he would need a hideaway where he could relax. He told his secretary, Lawrence Richey, that he was seeking a mountain

President Hoover, in suit and tie, fishes at Camp Rapidan in the summer of 1932. (HERBERT HOOVER LIBRARY)

site within 100 miles of Washington near a good trout stream. Hoover wanted the place to be at least 2,500 feet above sea level so mosquitoes would not be a problem.

Not long after he moved into the White House in March 1929, the location became known: a deep hollow on the eastern slope of the Blue Ridge. About seven miles west of the village of Criglersville, Virginia, it is where Laurel Prong and Mill Prong meet to form the Rapidan River. Camp Rapidan is what Hoover called it. Today it's Camp Hoover.

Once Mrs. Hoover had approved the site, a crew of several hundred marines set to work constructing a dozen cabins, barracks for 250 men, and riding stables. The president's cabin has a big-beamed living room with a stone fireplace, for which the marines carted in fifty-one tons of boulders. There is an adjoining dining area, two bedrooms, and a spacious porch that overlooks the trout streams.

A few Democrats complained about Hoover's use of tax dollars to create a 164-acre playground for himself. But Hoover answered the critics by pointing out that he personally paid $5 an acre, the going price, for the land, and also contributed $15,000 for construction materials.

Whenever it was possible for him to steal away, Hoover would motor out to Camp Rapidan, often spending the weekend there. Wearing hip boots, he would wade into the river and fish with a light trout rod and flies. He liked to fish alone.

After he left office, Hoover donated Camp Rapidan to the National Park Service and it became part of Shenandoah National Park. He hoped it would be used as a weekend retreat for presidents. But Franklin D. Roosevelt, who had overwhelmed Hoover in the election of 1932, found Camp Rapidan too remote. In 1942, he established a replacement—a presidential retreat in a heavily wooded area of the Catoctin Mountains of Maryland, about seventy miles from Washington. Roosevelt called it Camp Shangri-La, the name of the mountain kingdom in *Lost Horizon*, a novel by English author James Hilton. In 1945, President Harry Truman made Shangri-La the official presidential retreat. President Dwight D. Eisenhower gave the camp its present name in 1953, naming it Camp David after his grandson, David Eisenhower.

But Camp Rapidan, or Camp Hoover, as it is now known, has not been entirely forgotten. After Roosevelt abandoned the site, it served as a Boy Scout camp for many years. President Nixon was interested enough in Camp Hoover to have a helicopter pad built at Big Meadow, three miles from the site, but he never used it. Jimmy Carter, a devoted fisherman, made at least two visits to the camp.

Government officials occasionally use Camp Hoover on weekends. It is opened to the public once a year on the weekend nearest to August 10, Herbert Hoover's birthday.

When President Hoover first chose the site for the camp, the Department of Interior stocked the nearby rivers with trout so the presidents and his guests would be much less likely to have to endure any of the frustrations the average angler must suffer. The descendants of those trout swim in the Rapidan today, and are available to anyone with the necessary licenses and permits and, as Hoover himself once put it, the desire to "wash one's soul with pure air, with the rush of the brook, or with the shimmer of sun on blue water."

Of all the presidents who fished, Hoover was perhaps the most skilled. But he was a bit snobbish in his attitude toward the sport and the people who took part in it. In an article he wrote, "The Class Distinction Among Fishermen," Hoover put dry-fly fishermen at the top of the social order. Wet-fly casters and then spin casters followed. Those who used live bait were at the very bottom of the list.

Hoover wrote that among fishing presidents, only he, Theodore Roosevelt, and Grover Cleveland "had been life-

long fly fishermen before they went to the White House."
He sneered at Woodrow Wilson and Franklin D. Roosevelt
for going after the "common fishes." And he singled out Calvin Coolidge for failing to progress from worms to dry flies
during his years as president.

When it came to sports, Coolidge knew little and cared
less when he became president in 1923. But thanks to Edmund Starling, who was in charge of the White House Secret Service unit, Coolidge became skilled in a number of
outdoor activities during his presidency.

Fishing was one of them. One summer Coolidge vaca-
tioned at Lake Osgood in the Adirondack Mountains of
New York. There, Starling persuaded him to try fishing. The
Secret Service agent realized that Coolidge had probably
never fished before, not even during his boyhood years in
Vermont.

Coolidge had to be taught all the basics—how to bait his
hook and cast, how to hold the rod, how to handle the reel
and line, what to do when he got a bite. To Coolidge, the
whole thing seemed a little foolish. He couldn't understand
what people saw in the sport. But then he caught his first
fish—a five-pound pike—and his attitude changed completely. He wanted to do nothing but fish, and insisted on
going to the lake with Starling every day.

Coolidge and his wife spent the summer of 1927 at the
South Dakota State Game Lodge in the Black Hills. When
the president and Starling started off on their first fishing
expedition, they were surrounded by reporters and photographers. Coolidge mentioned to the press that he was not a
fly fisherman; he intended to use worms and grasshoppers
for bait.

Coolidge was unprepared for the furor that followed. To

During his tenure as president, from 1923 to 1929, Calvin Coolidge became skilled in several outdoor sports. Fishing was one of them. (THE CALVIN COOLIDGE MEMORIAL FOUNDATION)

fly fishermen, who considered the use of worms grossly un-sportsmanlike, the chief executive might as well have said he was going fishing with dynamite. "Worms!" blared a head-line in the *New York World*. "Words fail! Comment is use-less!" Politicians joined in the controversy. Said one senator: "There's no telling what a man will do who will catch trout with a worm."

Coolidge shrugged off the criticism. He wanted to catch fish, and the surest way to do it was with worms. Coolidge had been born in Vermont, and that was how Vermonters did it.

Later, Coolidge did become somewhat adept as a fly fish-erman. But it wasn't because of the criticism. One day when he and Starling were fishing an Adirondack stream, Starling caught several large trout with flies. Coolidge, who had used his trusty worms, went home empty-handed. The experience caused Coolidge to give fly-fishing a try. Starling taught him to cast. But during the long training period, Secret Service agents were kept busy removing hooks from trees, bushes, and even Coolidge's own clothing. Herbert Hoover or Jimmy Carter could have given this president a lesson or two.

CHAPTER 7

IN THE SADDLE

THE REAGANS NAMED IT RANCHO DEL CIELO—THEIR "ranch in the sky." Almost 700 acres of rugged land, the ranch is in the Santa Ynez Mountains of California, 2,200 feet above the Pacific Ocean and some 100 miles northeast of Los Angeles. To Nancy and Ronald Reagan, it became their ranch retreat, a mountain hideaway so remote only a handful of outsiders ever saw it. "This is where I restore myself," Reagan said.

During his years as president, Reagan was often flown to the ranch by helicopter from the Los Angeles airport. Otherwise, Rancho del Cielo was accessible only by climbing several torturous miles, preferably in a four-wheel-drive vehicle, over rutted roads, through steep-sided ravines, and around hairpin turns. The drive made Nancy Reagan nervous.

The ranch's five-room, century-old adobe house depended on two fireplaces for heat. In the mountains overlooking the ocean, a fire was needed at night, even in the summer. Reagan cut, hauled, and stacked the needed wood. He called it "good, solid, productive work," and from it he got a sense of accomplishment. A friend of Reagan's who knew about all of the chopping, hauling, and stacking said that Reagan should write a book about the fitness benefits he was getting and call it *Pumping Firewood*.

Reagan also stayed busy at the ranch by keeping the twelve miles of riding trails cleared of overgrowth, pruning trees and cutting brush. And there were also fences to be repaired. One summer Reagan and a ranch hand built 400 feet of fence out of old telephone poles. This involved cutting the posts and rails to size with a chain saw, notching the ends, and digging the holes. "It was tiring, heavy work," said Reagan, "but the exertion felt good, and we ended up with a handsome fence as well."

For recreation, there was horseback riding, which Reagan has enjoyed for most of his life, beginning in 1935. In that year he was twenty-four and working as the sports announcer at a Des Moines, Iowa, radio station; he joined the Fourteenth Cavalry Reserves as a second lieutenant so he could use the army horses at Fort Des Moines and do all the free riding he wanted. In the half century that followed, Reagan was never far from a ranch and horses.

"A lot of people don't realize what good exercise horseback riding is," Reagan said. "You just don't get on a horse and sit there as if you are in a deck chair. When that horse takes its first step, every muscle in your body reacts and moves with it. And the faster the horse moves, the more your muscles react." Reagan praised riding not only because it kept his muscles flexible, but also for its cardiovascular benefits—that is, for stimulating the heart and lungs.

But Reagan got more than physically fit from riding. He said, "Once you're up there on that horse, you get a different

President Reagan loved riding, and not only for its fitness benefits. "It's a tonic, really refreshing," he said. (RONALD REAGAN LIBRARY)

During his acting career, Reagan was happiest when doing outdoor movies that involved horses. *Stallion Road* was one. (COLLECTION OF HERMAN DARVICK)

perspective on life itself. It's a tonic, really refreshing." Reagan often quoted this old cavalry saying: "There's nothing as good for the inside of a man as the outside of a horse." Reagan said he believed the saying "wholeheartedly."

During his acting career, which spanned twenty-seven years and involved fifty-three films, Reagan was happiest when he was doing an outdoor movie on location rather than working at a studio soundstage. In one such film, *Sergeant Murphy,* released in 1938, Reagan played a private in the cavalry who is devoted to a horse with a gift for jumping. *Stallion Road,* a 1947 release in which Reagan played a ranch owner, was another favorite of his because it concerned horses. Coached by an Italian cavalry officer, Reagan did all his own riding and jumping in the film, without resorting to a stuntman.

In *The Last Outpost,* an adventure film that dates to 1951, Reagan played a Civil War cavalryman. Reagan was thrilled when he was permitted to use one of his own horses, named Tarbaby, in the movie. The production company shipped Tarbaby to Arizona where the movie was filmed. Tarbaby not only excelled as a "picture horse," but also won praises for the stamina she displayed in the Arizona heat. " 'Twas a proud moment for its owner," said Reagan.

In the years before he entered politics, Reagan rode several times a week. When he lived in the White House, his riding was limited to weekends at Camp David, although occasionally during the week he would get to use the riding trails at the Quantico marine base, a quick limousine ride across the Potomac River into northern Virginia.

When vacationing at Rancho del Cielo, President Reagan was usually at the horsebarn each morning by ten o'clock. There his favorite horse, Little Man, a Thoroughbred that Reagan had raised from a colt, would be waiting for him. (Little Man's mother was Tarbaby, the mare Reagan rode in *The Last Outpost.*) The Reagans' other horses included a chubby bay named No Strings, Nancy's favorite, and two Arabians, a white named Gualianko and a sorrel named Catalina.

Reagan liked to ride for a couple of hours each morning and do ranch chores in the afternoon. He saddled the horses himself, cleaned their hooves, and, in his younger days (Reagan was sixty-nine when he became president), even changed their shoes.

Reagan was rarely far from a ranch and horses. (RONALD REAGAN
LIBRARY)

Reagan grooms one of his horses at the stables at Rancho del Cielo.
(RONALD REAGAN LIBRARY)

Aboard the spirited Little Man, Reagan did mostly trail riding, making his way through heavily wooded stretches and across broad meadows. One problem with riding at Rancho del Cielo was that Reagan had to be followed closely by an army of mounted Secret Service agents and communications personnel. As he once noted, "A romantic ride with Nancy turns into a big stampede."

Several months after he had left the presidency, Reagan suffered minor injuries after being thrown by a horse. The accident took place in the Mexican state of Sonora (just across the Arizona border), where Reagan was vacationing. He was winding his way down a rocky slope when his mount bucked wildly. He hung on for a time, but the horse eventually stumbled, crashing him to the ground. He suffered cuts and bruises to his wrists and arms. Afterward, Reagan joked about the accident, saying it was "my own private rodeo."

The "rodeo," however, didn't dim Reagan's enthusiasm for riding. In his eighties and living in retirement in California, the former president continues to visit Rancho del Cielo for a few days every month, there to spend some time in the saddle.

Ronald Reagan's friends, noting how he loved riding and ranch life, sometimes kidded him by saying he was a frustrated cowboy. Reagan didn't mind the kidding. He realized there was a lot of truth in what they said.

Lyndon B. Johnson, a Texan, was another president who was comfortable on horseback. On vacations he would return to his LBJ Ranch, a 400-acre spread about sixty-five miles west of Austin. At the ranch, Johnson was fond of wearing Western-style clothes, complete with a ten-gallon hat. When he saddled up and went riding over his mesquite-covered land, it was sometimes because cameramen who were covering him had asked him to go on horseback. Johnson normally preferred to tour his ranch from behind the wheel of a sleek convertible.

Calvin Coolidge's interest in horseback riding led to an unusual adventure. During the summer of 1927, when Coolidge was vacationing in the Black Hills of South Dakota, he happened to get reintroduced to riding, an activity he had not tried since his boyhood days in Vermont. Colonel Edmund Starling, who also taught him to fish, saw to it that the president was assigned a very gentle mount. Named Mistletoe, the horse always traveled at a slow pace, and Coolidge rode daily without mishap.

When Coolidge returned to the White House, he found that an admirer, having heard of the president's interest in riding, had sent him a mechanical horse. Coolidge mounted the steed and pressed a button. Instantly, the horse shot, rocked, and bucked like a wild bronco, providing much more fun than Mistletoe ever had.

Coolidge began riding the mechanical horse every afternoon. Starling attended the sessions. The two men would take turns trying to cope with the endless stream of jolts and jerks, and their laughter echoed throughout the family quarters.

Despite his great weight—more than 300 pounds—William Howard Taft occasionally rode horseback for exercise. When Taft was governor of the Philippines in 1903, rumors circulated in Washington saying he had become ill. Elihu Root, the secretary of war, sent Taft a cable inquiring about his health.

Taft responded that his health was excellent and that he had, in fact, just completed a twenty-five-mile horseback ride. Root cabled back, "How is the horse?"

Teddy Roosevelt, who occupied the White House just before Taft, rode hard and often. He took great pleasure in brisk gallops on bitterly cold days, when Washington's bridle paths were covered with snow and ice. And on the summer's hottest days, he liked to canter ahead of his struggling Secret Service agents, many of whom found riding an alien sport.

Roosevelt's mastery in the saddle was no accident. Following a brief career in New York State politics, Roosevelt, then in his late twenties, decided to go out west and become

President Coolidge enjoyed riding not only real horses but a mechanical one as well. (LIBRARY OF CONGRESS)

a rancher. He invested $50,000 in a harsh chunk of land in the Dakota Badlands. At the beginning, Cowboy Teddy was hooted at by the veteran ranch hands. They looked upon the future president as a tenderfoot, an Eastern dude. And they called him Four Eyes because he wore glasses. Who ever heard of a cowboy wearing glasses?

But Teddy quickly won the respect and admiration of the cowpokes with his gutsiness. Often he would be in the saddle for days at a time, riding across the barren land in search of lost cattle. He herded wild horses, lassoed skittish steers, and even tried his hand at taming wild broncos. Roosevelt took some bad spills. In one fall, he cracked a rib; another time, he broke a bone in his shoulder. Both injuries caused him agonizing pain, but since the ranch was hundreds of miles from a doctor, Roosevelt simply gutted it out. The bones eventually healed by themselves.

After four years as a rancher, Roosevelt returned to New York. He was appointed president of the New York City Police Board and, in 1897, became assistant secretary of the navy under President William McKinley. He was serving in that post when America's war with Spain broke out in 1898.

With the nation at war, Roosevelt could not sit on the sidelines. He resigned from his desk job and, as a lieutenant colonel, organized the First U.S. Volunteer Cavalry by recruiting men from cattle ranches, mining camps, and law enforcement agencies in the Southwest. Nicknamed the Rough Riders, the colorful regiment captured the imagination of the American public.

The Rough Riders trained in San Antonio, Texas, and soon after embarked for Cuba. There Roosevelt led the Rough Riders on a bold charge up Kettle Hill at San Juan in the face of heavy fire to rout the Spanish. For his "gal-

President Theodore Roosevelt learned to ride as a Dakota rancher during the mid-1880s. (LIBRARY OF CONGRESS)

During the Spanish-American War, Roosevelt helped to organize the First U.S. Volunteer Cavalry, known popularly as the Rough Riders. (LIBRARY OF CONGRESS)

lantry in action," Roosevelt was promoted to brigadier general in the field. On his return to the United States, he was acclaimed as the nation's hero.

Elected vice president in 1900 at the age of forty-two, Roosevelt became the youngest president in the nation's history when President McKinley was assassinated in 1901. He served out that term and was reelected in 1904.

The nation had never experienced a president quite like Teddy Roosevelt. During the first years of his presidency, Roosevelt was invited to lead the Seventh Cavalry over the famous Chickamauga battlefield in Georgia. He was happy to accept. Astride a spirited army horse, Roosevelt paraded ahead of the other riders, who followed along in squadron formation. Then Roosevelt asked the colonel in charge to give the order "Forward, trot!" With Roosevelt setting the pace, the trot became a canter, and the canter became a gallop. The president kept in the lead, with the entire squadron thundering behind. A grove of pine trees appeared ahead. Roosevelt had no intention of slowing down. He plunged into the thicket of trees and tangled underbrush, lurching one way and then the other to make his way through. About a dozen riders were thrown from their horses and had to be treated for injuries. But Roosevelt came through without a scratch, grinning and waving. Afterward, he gave a brief speech in which he praised the men of the squadron for their excellent riding.

Roosevelt's adventures on horseback weren't always crowned with success. "The President came in this morning badly banged up about the head and face," Secretary of State John Hay wrote in his diary on October 23, 1904. "His horse fell on him yesterday." Several days later, Hay noted that the president had "landed . . . on his head, and his neck and shoulders were severely wrenched."

Ulysses S. Grant was another president who numbered horses among the great interests in his life. He liked to ride them, drive them, and talk about them. He once told a friend it was better to select your own hobby than to have one chosen for you by the newspapers. So Grant had selected horses. When anyone tried to bring up a topic that might prove embarrassing to him as the nation's leader, Grant would turn the conversation to horses. It was said that politicians would leave the White House grumbling that they could not get any information from Grant. "When I talk politics, he talks horses," said one.

Grant's interest in horses began during his early childhood. His father owned a tannery in Georgetown, Ohio, and was considered quite successful. He allowed his son to have his own horse at a very early age. Although Grant was small as a young boy, he proved to have exceptional skill in handling his horse, and most others as well. A sensitive boy, he also had a keen understanding of the animals. Neighboring farmers called upon young Ulysses to teach their horses to pace or trot, or to break their bad-tempered foals.

Once a circus came to town with a trick pony, trained to unseat its riders with violent jerks and bucks. During the circus performance, the ringmaster offered five dollars to any boy who could ride the pony. Several tried, but the colt quickly dumped them. Then came Ulysses's turn. Around and around the ring the pony raced, with Ulysses holding tightly to his back. Then the pony stopped abruptly and reared on his hind legs. Ulysses grasped the pony around the neck and held on for all he was worth. The pony shook and kicked but still could not throw the young rider.

The ringmaster had made up his mind that he was not going to lose the five dollars, so he put a monkey on the horse's back to rattle poor Ulysses. The monkey scampered up Ulysses's back, stood on his shoulders, and began to paw at his hair, while the horse continued to gallop around the ring. Although afraid of the pawing monkey, Ulysses clung

Of all the presidents, Ulysses S. Grant was perhaps the most
accomplished horseman. (LIBRARY OF CONGRESS)

to the horse. The crowd laughed and applauded. Ulysses rode on until the ringmaster handed him his five dollars in prize money.

In 1839, when he was seventeen, Grant entered the U.S. Military Academy at West Point. In those days, the academy had no organized sports to offer, except for fencing and riding. Grant was thus able to continue his devotion to horses. It wasn't long before he was being recognized as the academy's most skilled horseman. "It was as good as any circus to see Grant ride," said one of the cadets.

Grant excelled as a jumper and set a West Point jumping record that lasted for a quarter of a century. At the graduation exercises of the senior class, Grant executed a jump that remained in everyone's memory for years. "The riding master placed a leaping bar higher than a man's head and called out, 'Cadet Grant,' " wrote General J. B. Fry. "A clean-faced, slender, blue-eyed young fellow weighing about 120 pounds dashed from the ranks on a powerfully built sorrel and galloped down the opposite side of the hall. As he came into the stretch, the horse increased his pace and, measuring his stride for the great leap before him, bounded into the air and cleared the bar, carrying his rider as if man and beast had been welded together. The spectators were breathless."

Three years after Grant graduated from West Point, war flared between the United States and Mexico. It lasted until 1848. Grant fought in several battles. At the battle of Monterey, he added luster to his reputation as a horseman. Clinging to the side of his horse, he galloped through enemy fire to an ammunition wagon and retrieved a fresh supply of powder and bullets for besieged troops. Grant was cited for bravery and promoted to the rank of captain.

Grant not only got great pleasure from riding but also en-

The Grant children, girls as well as boys, were skilled riders, too.
(LIBRARY OF CONGRESS)

joyed driving horses, and frequently during his life owned
fast-stepping trotters. This was the case when he lived in
Washington, D.C., following the Civil War and, later, during
the two terms of his presidency. Grant had the White House

stables rebuilt to accommodate the dozen or so horses he acquired to drive. One day as he sped along M Street not far from the White House, Grant was arrested for fast driving. When the officer realized he had apprehended the president, he became speechless. Grant was more amused than angry. "Officer, do your duty," he said. While the officer brought his horse and carriage to the police station, Grant walked back to the White House.

Grant's affection for horses lasted throughout his life. In his years of retirement, Grant lived in New York City, where he drove fast trotters along Harlem Lane, then one of the city's main thoroughfares. Grant died in 1885 at the age of sixty-three.

George Washington probably spent more time in the saddle than any other president, including Ulysses S. Grant. When Washington was a young man, his horses carried him on long surveying expeditions in the Shenandoah Valley of northern Virginia. Later, they took him through the thick woods and across the rolling meadows of Mount Vernon on inspection tours and frenzied foxhunts, and they bore him into battle in two wars. The famous writer Washington Irving once said of Washington, "If there was anything he was likely to take pride in, it was horses; he was passionately fond of that noble animal."

Of Washington's many horses, a big, fast sorrel stallion named Nelson was said to be his favorite. Nelson was the horse that Washington rode during the Revolutionary War. He counted on Nelson to be steady and calm during the din and turmoil of battle.

After the war, Washington frequently rode a white parade horse named Prescott. While Prescott was not disturbed by the waving of banners or the clamor of marching bands, the

A youthful George Washington gives a young horse its first lessons.
(LIBRARY OF CONGRESS)

stallion had the habit of shaking and bobbing about whenever a carriage drew near. This was an embarrassment to
Washington, who sought to ride as quietly as possible.

At one time, Washington stabled as many as 140 horses at
Mount Vernon. The saddle horses were groomed with the
greatest care. The night before they were to be ridden, the
horses were covered with a white paste, then wrapped in
body cloths. The paste hardened during the night and the
next morning it was rubbed into the horses' coats before
they were curried and brushed. The treatment made the
coats lustrous. In addition, the horses' hooves were
scrubbed, blackened, and polished; their mouths were
washed; and their teeth were picked and cleaned.

Horses remained an interest of Washington's throughout
his life. Gilbert Stuart, a noted artist who painted memorable
portraits of Washington, once recalled, "I found that it was
difficult to interest him in conversation while I was taking
his portrait. I began on the Revolution—the battles of Mon-
mouth and Princeton—but he was absolutely dumb. After a
while I got on horses. Then I touched the right chord."

CHAPTER 8

ON THE GRIDIRON

D UTCH WAS WHAT YOU'D CALL AN AVERAGE PLAYER," Ralph McKinzie, coach of the Eureka (Illinois) College Red Devils, once remarked. "He was not a star, but he was very conscientious and dedicated and worked very hard.

"I can remember after practice he'd pull out a broom handle or something and pretend it was a microphone and start broadcasting the game we played the week before—names, players, everything. Just as real as it could be. The kids would stop dressing just to listen to it.

"I thought broadcasting was the career he'd follow. But danged if he didn't become president."

The player Coach McKinzie was talking about was Ronald Reagan, a sports broadcaster and then a Hollywood actor, who, in 1981, became the fortieth president. Reagan was known as "Dutch" during his college days and earlier.

At Eureka College, which is in central Illinois about twenty miles from Peoria, Reagan was involved in many different activities. He was a reporter for the school paper, a member of the drama society, and president of the school senate; he also worked on the yearbook staff. When it came to sports, Reagan earned letters in swimming, track, and football.

Reagan was never a star with the football team. Coach Mac admired his skills as a blocker and tackler and made Reagan the team's starting guard halfway through his sophomore season.

"He always had a lot of fight and spirit," said Coach Mac. "And he was always an unselfish player. He wasn't one who tried to glorify himself at the expense of others. He was a team player all the way. He knew a team, by God, is a machine, and every player is a cog in the machine."

There are two athletic monuments on the tiny, tree-lined campus of Eureka. One is the football field named for Coach McKinzie in 1933; he died in 1990, at the age of ninety-six. The other is the gymnasium that bears the former president's name. Reagan's name was added in 1971, while he was governor of California.

Ronald Reagan's years as a varsity football player at Eureka College gave an important boost to his acting career. Early in the 1940s, after Reagan had made some twenty movies for Warner Brothers, all of them "B" pictures—that is, films that were second best in terms of quality and importance—Reagan learned that the studio was soon to begin filming *Knute Rockne, All American*, the life story of the legendary football coach at the University of Notre Dame. Pat O'Brien, a major star of the time, was to play Rockne.

A major film, Reagan realized, could provide him with an escape from "B" films. The role Reagan wanted was that of George Gipp. As a sports announcer at WHO in Des Moines, Reagan had told his audiences about the fabled Gipp—how he had run eighty yards through the Notre

Ronald Reagan plays touch football with his son, Ron Junior, in the backyard of their home in Sacramento. Reagan was governor of California at the time. (WIDE WORLD)

Dame varsity the first time he was handed a football, one of his many glittering moments as a backfield star for the Fighting Irish.

Two weeks before his final game at Notre Dame, Gipp died of pneumonia. On his deathbed, Gipp is said to have told Rockne: "Someday when things are tough, maybe you can tell the boys to go out there and win one for the Gipper." At the end of the movie, when Notre Dame seemed on the

Reagan's all-time favorite acting role was that of George Gipp—the famed "Gipper"—in the film biography of Knute Rockne. (COLLECTION OF HERMAN DARVICK)

brink of losing to its archrival Army, Rockne, in an emotional halftime appeal, electrified the team by calling upon the players to "win one for the Gipper." (In his years as president, Reagan often made use of the phrase, which he always delivered with a wide smile.)

Reagan thought he would be perfect as Gipp, but the studio had its doubts. Several other actors were tested for the part, and all proved unsatisfactory. They were told they didn't look like football players.

Reagan, however, would not accept being rejected. He showed the film's producers photographs of himself in a Eureka football uniform and explained that he was skilled and experienced in every phase of the sport. He also got Pat O'Brien to put in a word for him. Eventually, Reagan got the part.

Knute Rockne, All American has been described as one of the best films about sports ever made. While Reagan in the role of George Gipp is on the screen for only a relatively short time, his acting was never better. Reagan had always been described as a pleasing and capable actor, but never much more than that. Reviews of the Rockne film, however, hailed him for his warmth, his dramatic appeal, and the feeling of reality he was able to convey. Among his scores of roles, that of George Gipp was Reagan's favorite.

The movie did wonders for Reagan's career. He said, "It was the springboard that bounded me into a wider variety of parts in pictures." He also began receiving offers to play roles of better quality. "Upper-crust picture making" is what Reagan called it.

Some of the criticism he got bothered Reagan, however. He considered it unfair. He said, "One sportswriter wondered why producers never picked real football players for such parts. As I practically earned my way through college playing football, that disturbed me."

But Reagan also received some unmerited praise. Another sportswriter praised him for being so accurate in his portrayal of George Gipp that he even imitated the slight limp he had. "Actually," said Reagan, "I wasn't trying to limp. I just wasn't used to my new football shoes and my feet hurt."

THREE PRESIDENTS BESIDES RONALD REAGAN WERE VARSITY football players in college. Gerald Ford was a lineman at the

Dick Nixon, a member of the second-string football team at Whittier College. (WIDE WORLD)

University of Michigan. Of all the football-playing presidents, Ford was probably the best. Richard Nixon was a 155-pound reserve at Whittier College in California. Dwight Eisenhower was a halfback at the U.S. Military Academy at West Point, but a knee injury cut short his football career.

John F. Kennedy and Franklin D. Roosevelt were would-be football players. Both tried out for football at Harvard. But both lacked size and failed to win varsity status.

Other presidents were closely associated with football, although not as players. Herbert Hoover, while at Stanford University, played a role in setting up the first intercollegiate football game on the West Coast. Both Woodrow Wilson, who coached the sport, and Teddy Roosevelt had an important influence on the game's rules and regulations.

Gerald Ford's connection with football began when he was very young. When he went to kindergarten at Madison Elementary School in Grand Rapids, Michigan, Ford played pickup games on empty lots. "Even at that age," Ford said in his autobiography, *A Time to Heal*, "I recall . . . coming home with a dirty face, torn clothes, and skinned knees and elbows."

For South High School in Grand Rapids, Ford played center on a city championship team. The center is the player in the middle of the line whose job it is to snap the ball back between his legs to the quarterback, running back, or punter.

Football teams nowadays use the T formation, and the center merely has to hand the ball back between his legs to the quarterback, who's standing right behind him. The center is able to look straight ahead and deliver his block as he snaps the ball. But in Ford's time, when teams used the single-wing or double-wing formations, playing center was quite different. The back who was to receive the ball lined up several yards behind the center. That meant the center had to bend over and look between his legs at the back. He saw everything upside down.

This gave the opposing linemen a big advantage. They could launch their attack while the center was bent over and looking through his legs. "You had to be very quick," Ford once said. Indeed.

A star as a high school center, Ford was pursued by several major colleges, including Michigan, Michigan State, and Northwestern. He chose Michigan. As a sophomore and junior, Ford played second string on an undefeated team that won the national championship two years in a row. As a senior and a first-string player, he was named the team's most valuable player and participated in the all-star game the following summer against the Chicago Bears, pro champions at the time. (The Bears won, 5–0.)

Each college player received $100. Ford had been accepted at Yale Law School, and he used his $100 to pay his transportation to New Haven, Connecticut, where Yale is located.

In 1948, when he was thirty-five, Ford was elected to Congress, launching the political career that eventually led to the presidency. "Looking back, I realized I was lucky to have competed in sports," Ford said in his autobiography. "As a football player, you have critics in the stands and critics in the press. Few of them have ever centered a ball, kicked a punt, or thrown a touchdown pass with 100,000 people looking on, yet they assume they know all the answers. Their comments helped me to develop a thick hide, and in later years whenever critics assailed me, I just let their jibes roll off my back."

A center, Gerald Ford starred for the University of Michigan in the mid-1930s. (UNIVERSITY OF MICHIGAN)

Gerald Ford and Ronald Reagan gave up football after college. Jack Kennedy, on the other hand, played the game through most of his life, despite the fact that his bad back caused him serious and frequent pain. His back condition also meant that anytime he was the victim of a block or tackle he was in danger of critical injury.

Kennedy first played football in grade school at Dexter, a private academy. As a teenager, Kennedy, pale and very thin at the time, went out for the football team at his prep school but never managed to earn varsity status.

Later, at Harvard, Kennedy sought to become an end. "Jack wouldn't be considered a top-notch player because he lacked weight and swiftness," said Torbert MacDonald, Kennedy's college roommate (and later a congressman from Massachusetts). "However, he practiced diligently and made the most of his natural talents. And he was very determined."

As a sophomore, Kennedy was a member of the junior varsity. One afternoon while scrimmaging against the heavier, more experienced varsity squad, Kennedy severely wrenched his back; the injury put an end to his college football career.

But Kennedy never abandoned the game completely. In 1940, as a young U.S. Navy ensign stationed in Washington, D.C., Kennedy would turn out every Sunday afternoon for the touch football games on the Mall, near the Washington Monument. And later, while serving in Congress, he would occasionally slip out of his office early, change into a sweatshirt or old sweater, and hurry over to a playground in nearby Georgetown to run plays with a group of high school boys. Certainly none of them ever realized that their tall, slender teammate was to become the president of the United States one day.

Touch football was the large Kennedy family's game of choice, although it was scarcely a game. It was serious business. Bobby Kennedy once said, "Except for war, there is nothing in American life—nothing—that trains a boy better for life than football."

Teams of Kennedys would battle one another in ferocious nonstop touch football games on the sloping lawns of Hyannisport, the Kennedy family compound near the town of Hyannis on Cape Cod. Kennedy sisters, wives, and in-laws were expected to join in and play with the same grim determination as the men.

Injuries were shrugged off. At various times, Bobby Kennedy played with a fractured leg and a dislocated shoulder. The future president did not get off unscathed. On the day before his marriage to Jacqueline Bouvier, Kennedy hurtled into a clump of rosebushes while trying to get his hands on a long pass. At the wedding the next day, the scratches that resulted could be seen on his face.

His bride suffered more. Not long after their marriage, she broke her ankle in one of the family games. After that, she never played again.

Injuries have to be expected now and then in such a rough sport as football. Dwight Eisenhower, the president who held office just before Jack Kennedy, had been a promising athlete, a member of the varsity football team at West Point in 1912. But an injury cut short his career.

When young Eisenhower, who was nicknamed Ike, entered Abilene High School in Abilene, Kansas, the school had no athletic program, no money for coaches, and no money for equipment. The students who wanted to play sports formed the Abilene High School Association to raise the needed funds. Eisenhower was elected president of the organization. By collecting donations from local citizens, the boys managed to accumulate enough money to buy equipment and uniforms for both baseball and football.

Eisenhower starred in both sports. In baseball, he played right field and was the team's best hitter. In football, he was a tackle. Everyone played "both ways" in those days—that is, both offense and defense. When Ike's team had the ball, he was quick and powerful enough to open holes for the ball carrier. On defense, he was a fierce tackler.

After Ike graduated from high school, he went to work in a creamery. But he also returned to high school in the fall to take some more courses. Since there were no rules that prevented graduates from playing football, Eisenhower joined the team for another season.

By this time, Ike had decided he wanted to further his education, but his family could not afford to send him to college. The military academies were Eisenhower's solution to that problem. Both the U.S. Military Academy at West Point and the U.S. Naval Academy at Annapolis offered free room and board and tuition.

In Eisenhower's time, a candidate took a War Department entrance examination for both academies. Since Ike had no real preference between the two academies, he simply put down "either" on his application form in the space where he was asked to indicate his choice. He saw nothing wrong with letting the government make the decision for him.

Ike did well on the examination. Deep down, he hoped to be appointed to the naval academy. But the naval academy, as he later learned, would not accept any candidate older than nineteen, and Ike was twenty. In the summer of 1911,

Eisenhower arrived at West Point, ready to begin his freshman year.

It wasn't long before he began to make a name for himself, not only in football but in baseball, boxing, and track as well. As a sophomore, he began the season as the Army team's second-string left halfback. As he had been in high school, Ike was a two-way player. On offense, he was a ball carrier; on defense, he backed up the line. He also punted.

Just before Army's first game of the season, against Stevens, Geoffrey Keyes, the starting left halfback and one of the team's stars the year before, was injured during a practice session. Ike was called upon to take over. The cadets and their supporters feared that the loss of Keyes would hurt their chances. But Ike delivered. He knifed his way through the Stevens line for long gains and flattened any ball carrier who penetrated the Army line. Army won, 27–0.

The next week, with Rutgers furnishing the opposition, and Keyes still out of the lineup, Eisenhower put on a repeat performance, leading the cadets to a 19–0 win. Sportswriters began to take notice. One called Eisenhower the "Kansas Cyclone." The *New York Times* hailed him as "one of the most promising backs in Eastern football."

In the weeks that followed, Army lost to Yale, 6–0, then swept past Colgate, 18–7. The next week Army faced Carlisle Indian School. Known as the Indians, the mighty Carlisle squad was led by Jim Thorpe, the famed Sauk and Fox Indian who was one of the greatest athletes ever. After his brilliant college career, Thorpe played professional football and also major league baseball. He won gold medals in the pentathlon and decathlon in the 1912 Olympic Games. On the football field, Thorpe did everything—block, tackle, pass, and carry the ball. When playing Carlisle, every team

By his second year at West Point, Cadet Eisenhower was on his way to football stardom. (U.S. MILITARY ACADEMY)

had the same game plan: "Stop Thorpe." But he was practically unstoppable.

Against Army, Thorpe was at the top of his game. He tore big holes in the Army line and skirted the ends for long chunks of yardage. On one of his romps, Eisenhower and a teammate ganged up on Thorpe. Ike hit him low, around the ankles. The other player went in high, tackling Thorpe around the waist. Thorpe hit the ground hard, and when he got up he was dazed and groggy. Ike thought that he and his teammate had finally tamed Thorpe. But the very next play, he bolted through the Army line for a ten-yard gain.

There was no stopping Thorpe that afternoon. The game ended with Carlisle on top, 27–6. At the final gun, the entire corps of cadets stood and filled the air with resounding cheers for Thorpe. As for poor Eisenhower, he limped slowly from the field, having suffered a painful knee injury.

Ike rested his injured knee and was in the lineup the following Saturday, when Army played Tufts University, winning, 15–6. Midway through the game, Eisenhower's weakened knee suddenly gave way. He collapsed and had to be carried from the field.

Dr. Charles Keller, the chief surgeon at the U.S. Military Academy, examined the knee. Ike, although in great pain, asked whether he would be able to play in the Navy game. "Not this year," the doctor said. "Maybe never."

Eisenhower spent several weeks in the hospital with his leg in a cast. The injury proved so serious that he was not able to play football again. His career had come to an abrupt end. It was one of the bitterest disappointments of his life.

During his remaining years at West Point, Ike tried to stay close to football by coaching a freshman team. But it was hard for him to put what happened out of his mind. His teammates were aware of how he felt. The 1915 edition of the *Howitzer*, an academy publication, described Ike in these terms: "Poor Dwight merely consents to exist until graduation shall set him free. At one time he threatened to get interested in life and won his 'A' by being the most promising back in Eastern football—but the Tufts game broke his knee and the promise."

During his long and distinguished career as a military leader, and later as president, Eisenhower continued to follow the ups and downs of the Army football team. Even when stationed in remote corners of the globe, he would make an effort to find out how the cadets had fared each Saturday afternoon. News of an Army victory never failed to bring a wide smile to his face.

After Eisenhower became president in 1953, his obvious affection for Army football threatened to cause an embarrassing incident whenever Army played its traditional rival, Navy. Eisenhower—as president, the commander in chief of *all* the armed forces—was supposed to remain neutral for the game. But how could someone with a lifelong devotion to the Army team be expected to be impartial?

Eisenhower sought to still any criticism from Navy's backers by sitting with the midshipmen on the Navy side of the stadium for half the game. Then, at halftime, the crowd would watch as Eisenhower left his seat and made his way across the field to sit among the cadets for the second half. Despite this display of nonpartisanship, no one doubted how Eisenhower really felt.

He provided evidence of his true sentiments before the 1958 Army-Navy contest. He sent a telegram to the Navy team carrying his "best personal wishes." He then sent a telegram to the Army squad, explaining what he told Navy and adding: "The requirements of neutrality are thus scrupulously observed. But over a span of almost half a century, on the day of The Game, I have only one thought and only one song: 'On, brave old Army team.' "

While Ronald Reagan, Gerald Ford, and Dwight D. Eisenhower enjoyed playing football during their college years, Woodrow Wilson, the twenty-eighth president, preferred to coach it. The role of teacher came naturally to him. Wilson spent three decades in academia, first as a college student, then as a professor, and finally as a university president, before being thrust into the world of politics.

Frail and with poor eyesight as a young man, Wilson first tried playing sports before he turned to coaching. As a seventeen-year-old freshman at Davidson College in North Carolina, Tommy, as he was called—his full name was Thomas Woodrow Wilson—played center field for the college baseball team. While he had passable skills, he was criticized for his lack of enthusiasm. "Tommy Wilson would be a good player if he wasn't so lazy," his coach said.

Perhaps young Wilson actually had more serious problems, physical problems. Poor health kept him at home for what would have been his sophomore year. In 1875, he transferred to Princeton, where he was named president of the baseball association. Later, as a professor at Princeton, he delighted in watching what he described as "the splendid games between the crack professional nines of the country."

But it was football that became his greatest interest. The very first college game had been played on November 6, 1869, only a few years before Wilson arrived at Princeton. Teams from Princeton and Rutgers battled one another. But the game didn't look like the version that's played today.

Passing and running weren't allowed. The ball could be advanced only with the foot, head, or shoulder.

Nor did teams have coaches in those days. Princeton, for example, was coached by a committee of students. Wilson showed such enthusiasm for football's technical aspects that he was elected to the coaching committee.

Football of the 1870s resembled British rugby in that the ball was put in play by means of a scrummage, or scrum. In scrum, the ball was rolled between the front lines of the two opposing teams. Each then tried to kick the ball back to a teammate.

Wilson and his fellow coaches argued against the scrum. They wanted one team to be given possession of the ball and be permitted to snap it back to start a play. This system, they declared, would make it possible for each team to have organized plays and a specific assignment for each offensive player.

Before long, the scrummage was discarded and the new system accepted. By that time, Wilson had moved on to Wesleyan University in Connecticut, where he had taken a post as a professor of history. But he still maintained his interest in football. Every afternoon following classes, he would appear at the practice field to help the team prepare for its upcoming game.

Wilson was credited with introducing a series of "rotation plays" at Wesleyan that the team used with great success. Similar to the no-huddle hurry-up offense made popular by professional football's Buffalo Bills in the late 1980s and early 1990s, the rotation system called for the team to run a fast sequence of several plays without pausing to call signals. When Wesleyan defeated Pennsylvania in 1889, much of the credit went to Professor Wilson and his clever play-calling.

Wilson was also the team's chief booster. He once scolded the Wesleyan fans for not supporting the team with loud enough cheers. Another time the seemingly quiet, mild-mannered Wilson charged out onto the field during a game to loudly protest a referee's decision.

Wilson returned to Princeton in the fall of 1890 as a professor of economy and jurisprudence. His coaching days came to an end that year when he was appointed chairman of the Committee on Outdoor Sports. In this role, he worked to improve Princeton's athletic program, supervising the building of new playing fields and training facilities. Wilson became Princeton's president in 1902.

During these years, Wilson must have been distressed to observe what was happening to his beloved sport of football: It had become a brutal game. Slugging, kicking, and gouging were common.

Injuries were frequent and some deaths occurred. During the season of 1905, a Harvard player sustained a cracked skull, and a Columbia lineman suffered partial blindness and had to drop out of school. A Pennsylvania player died from a kick in the head. The *Chicago Tribune* reported that during 1905 there were eighteen deaths and 159 serious injuries in high school and college football combined.

Everyone agreed the terrible violence had to stop. A newspaper suggested that colleges substitute soccer for football. Columbia University announced it was dropping football, and Harvard said it was about to do the same. It seemed likely that the game would vanish from the American scene.

President Theodore Roosevelt was well aware what was happening. Although he had never played the game himself, he felt that there were few better sports. Two of his sons, Ted and Kermit, played football at prep school. "I greatly

admire football," Roosevelt wrote to Ted in 1903, telling him
it was the ideal sport for developing "the simple but all-
essential traits which go to make up manliness."

The rugged nature of the game was what appealed to Roosevelt. Every player should bear down and sweat blood from
the opening kickoff to the final gun, he believed. In the advice he gave to America's young people, Roosevelt chose
football terms: "Don't flinch, don't foul, hit the line hard!"

When Roosevelt heard that some colleges were abandoning the sport because of increasing violence, it pained him.
He believed that football could be very helpful in building a
boy's character. He did not want the sport put on the shelf.
Rather, he felt, football must rid itself of the brutality that
had been allowed to flourish.

Roosevelt not only spoke out in favor of the sport, he
acted. In 1905, he invited representatives from the leading
colleges to a White House conference on the subject. At the
meeting, the president pounded the table with his fist and
told the colleges to change the game's rules and regulations
so that football could survive.

As a result of the conference, the American Football Rules
Committee was formed. The following year, 1906, new rules
were adopted that were meant to open up the game and
make it safer. Mass formations, which had contributed to
the violence, were banned. The distance to be gained on
downs to earn a first down was increased from five yards to
ten yards and the forward pass was introduced.

As a result of the changes, injuries were sharply cut. In
addition, football became more fun to play and more inter-
esting to watch.

Before the rule revisions, football was dominated by teams
with big men. They used their size and strength to over-

In the early 1900s, serious injuries and even deaths keynoted football. Theodore Roosevelt helped get colleges to change the rules and make the game safer. (NEW YORK PUBLIC LIBRARY)

power smaller teams. But the rule changes evened the playing field. Smaller teams, using the forward pass, could now compete on even terms against teams of big men. No longer was size as critical a factor in achieving football success.

It may seem odd that Roosevelt, who boosted football so enthusiastically and had such an important influence on the sport, never played it. The reason he never did had to do with his health. As a boy, Roosevelt suffered from asthma, which weakened him. When he entered Harvard, just before his eighteenth birthday, he was skinny, with pipestem legs, and was simply too frail for football. Although he didn't play football, Roosevelt rowed, hiked, wrestled, boxed, and traveled to Africa and South America to hunt big game. Only a small handful of presidents have been as physically active as Teddy Roosevelt.

CHAPTER 9

BASEBALL:
PRESIDENTIAL PASTIME

NͭOT LONG AFTER NOON ON APRIL 12, 1993, PRESIDENT BILL Clinton left the White House by limousine, traveling some thirty-five miles northeast to Baltimore—and Oriole Park at Camden Yards. There he was to throw out the ceremonial first ball of the baseball season, continuing a tradition that had been going on for almost a century.

Before the game, wearing an Oriole warm-up jacket over a bulletproof vest, Clinton strolled and chatted with players. After the playing of the national anthem, the stadium announcer told the sellout crowd: "Here to throw out the first ball is a rookie who's just moved into the area from Arkansas, the President of the United States, Bill Clinton." Both cheers and boos followed. Clinton jogged to a spot in front of the mound and tossed a soft left-handed pitch to the Baltimore catcher, Chris Hoiles.

After the pitch, the president visited the WMAR–TV broadcast booth. There he joined announcers Brooks Robinson, a Hall of Fame third baseman for the Orioles, and Jon Miller in calling the top half of the first inning. The president

President Clinton jokes with Baltimore catcher Chris Hoiles after tossing out the first pitch of the 1993 baseball season. (WIDE WORLD)

stayed until the seventh inning, then left for the return trip to the White House.

Baseball and American presidents have been closely identified since the end of the 1860s, when the sport was first hailed as America's "national pastime." Throwing out the first pitch on opening day is only one of several ways presi-

dents have been linked with the sport. Most presidents have
at least been fans. Abraham Lincoln, for example, watched
games between local Washington teams. Andrew Johnson,
who acceded to the presidency following Lincoln's assassination, attended a two-game series between the Philadelphia
Athletics and Washington Nationals in August 1865. The
games were played on White Lot, an enormous open area
south of the Executive Mansion.

Several chief executives—George Bush, Dwight Eisenhower, and William Howard Taft among them—were highly
skilled as players. Bush, a first baseman, captained a team at
Yale University that played for the college championship.

Taft was the president who originated the practice of
throwing out the first baseball of the season. The date was
April 10, 1910. The Washington Senators faced the Philadelphia Athletics at National Park. Taft decided to attend the
game on the spur of the moment, and the head umpire, Billy
Evans, suggested that the president throw out the first ball.
Taft thus established a tradition that has been followed by
every chief executive with the exception of Jimmy Carter.
Carter, a softball player, attended only one baseball game as
president.

When it comes to opening-day pitches, the all-time leader
is Franklin D. Roosevelt, who had eight. Of course, Roosevelt had more opportunities than anyone else. The nation's
only four-term president, Roosevelt occupied the Executive
Mansion for twelve opening days. His 1940 throw might be
regarded as a wild pitch: He smashed the camera of a *Washington Post* photographer.

Harry Truman, with seven opening days to his credit, is
second to Roosevelt. But for entertainment value, Truman

Franklin D. Roosevelt threw out eight opening-day first balls—more than any other president. (WIDE WORLD)

was hard to top. In both 1950 and 1951, he threw one ball right-handed and then another lefty.

Ronald Reagan, who attended two openers in his eight years as president, impressed fans with his strong right arm. It made some observers recall that Reagan did, after all, play the role of Grover Cleveland Alexander in the 1952 movie *The Winning Team*. Alexander won 373 games during his long major league career, including three seasons in which he won thirty or more. Reagan's association with baseball also included the five years he spent as a broadcaster of Chicago Cubs games.

Often the fans boo politicians at baseball games, and presidents usually don't escape at least some cries of disapproval. Once, before a game at Cincinnati's Riverfront Stadium, George Bush figured out a way to assure he wouldn't get booed. An eight-year-old girl and a twelve-year-old boy were supposed to go out onto the field before Bush. The president walked over to where the little girl was standing, smiled, bent down, and said to her, "Are you nervous? . . . Why don't we walk out together?" Bush realized that nobody would boo an eight-year-old girl and a twelve-year-old Little Leaguer. "It was a little bit defensive on my part," Bush said after. "But it worked."

In his years as president, Bush went to games when he could, often inviting heads of state or heads of government to go with him. He took President Hosni Mubarak of Egypt to a Baltimore game in 1989 and took England's Queen Elizabeth II to see the Orioles in 1990. He invited President Carlos Salinas de Gortari of Mexico to the All-Star Game in 1992.

As president, Bush threw out the first pitch on four opening days in three different cities—Baltimore, Toronto, and Arlington, Texas. Pitcher Nolan Ryan, who retired in 1993 after twenty-seven major league seasons and 324 victories, and who is a baseball friend of Bush's, once gave the president this advice for throwing out the first ball from the pitcher's mound: "Throw it high," Ryan said, "because amateurs get out there and throw it in the dirt. But if you heave it over the catcher's head, the crowd goes 'Ooooh' and 'Aaaah.' "

Bush, however, was not always able to follow Ryan's ad-

Bush put lots of effort into throwing out the ceremonial first pitch at New York's Shea Stadium in 1985. He was vice president at the time. (WIDE WORLD)

vice. On opening day in Baltimore in 1992, Bush was supposed to throw the ball from the mound to Oriole catcher Chris Hoiles. But Bush's toss bounced in the dirt and he threw his hands over his head in embarrassment. "That was the worst toss I've ever seen in my life," Hoiles declared. The weak toss wasn't completely his fault, Bush said later. He claimed he was hindered by the bulky bulletproof vest he was made to wear under his suit jacket.

Bush had a wider and deeper connection with baseball than any other president. There is, in fact, a baseball tradition in the Bush family. His father, Prescott Bush, played at Yale, as did an uncle. Assorted sons and grandsons of the Bushes have been Little Leaguers. And one son, George Junior, is a part owner of the Texas Rangers.

Growing up in Greenwich, Connecticut, the future president was an avid fan of the Boston Red Sox and followed the game very closely. He could spout off the averages of the top twenty hitters in both the American and National leagues. Bush played first base on his prep school team and enjoyed two championship seasons at Yale. In later life, he continued to play the game at his Kennebunkport vacation home.

New York Yankee first baseman Lou Gehrig, who played in 2,130 consecutive games to establish the greatest game-playing streak of all time, was Bush's boyhood hero. One of young Bush's plans was to write to Gehrig and ask him for his mitt, but somehow George never did so. Years later, Bush, as president, visited the locker room of the Los Angeles Dodgers following a game at Dodger Stadium, and pitcher Orel Hershiser showed Bush his glove. "It had Orel's name stitched along the thumb," Bush recalled. "I

George Bush captained the 1948 Yale baseball team. (YALE UNIVERSITY)

suddenly remembered Lou Gehrig's glove and how much I wanted it."

Bush was something of an oddity as a player. A natural left-hander, he threw left but batted right. "I was all inverted," he once said, "just backwards." Among natural lefties, only a very few have become good righty hitters. Bush was not one of the exceptions. But fielding was a different story: He excelled. As Junie O'Brien, a teammate of Bush's at Yale, once recalled, "The key thing about Poppy—as everyone called him—was that he was so sure-gloved. All the infielders knew that if they threw the ball anywhere near him, he was going to pull it in."

Before Yale, at Phillips Academy, better known as Andover after the Massachusetts town in which it is located, Bush was both a smooth-fielding first baseman and star of the soccer team. His exploits on the soccer field as the team's center forward caused one observer to write, "Poppy Bush's play throughout the season ranked him as one of Andover's all-time greats."

After he entered Yale in 1945, Bush played one season of soccer and then decided to concentrate on baseball. With World War II veterans returning to college—Bush had been a navy pilot in the South Pacific during the war—there was plenty of competition. Several of the members of Yale teams for which Bush played went on to careers in professional baseball, three of them in the major leagues.

Bush beat out the other candidates for first base with his splendid glove work. "He was excellent—a one-handed star," the Yale coach Ethan Allen once said. Well aware of his weakness as a hitter, Bush worked hard to improve. He hit the ball off a tee, and worked on hitting the ball where it was pitched and on hitting to all fields. In his first at-bat in a

Yale uniform, playing against the University of Connecticut, Bush drilled a single.

According to statistics issued by Yale, Bush hit .239 as a junior, .264 as a senior, and had a .251 career average, with two home runs in the fifty-one games in which he played. Once, in a game against North Carolina, Bush went three for five. His hits included a double and a triple. "Afterward," Bush recalls, "the scouts came running up to Ethan Allen. 'Hey, who is this kid?' they wanted to know. But when they looked at my averages, they went away."

While there may be some debate over his career batting average, there is no disputing the fact that Bush was one of the team's most popular players, if not *the* most popular. "He was just like a regular guy. Always friendly. A wonderful guy," said Norm Felske, the Yale team's catcher. "If you ate spaghetti, he ate spaghetti." The Yale team often traveled by train, and on such trips Bush led the singing or organized team gin rummy games. He was always kidding his teammates. Once, after Red Mathews had belted a home run and returned to the dugout to receive high fives and backslaps from his teammates, Poppy said to him, "Hey, Red, why don't you hit the ball next time?"

For his leadership qualities, Bush was elected team captain in 1948, his senior year. In both 1947 and 1948, the Yale team won the eastern championship and went to Kalamazoo, Michigan, to play in the National Collegiate Athletic Association (NCAA) finals. Both times they lost, once to California, the other time to Southern California.

In the years that he served as Ronald Reagan's vice president, from 1981 to 1989, Bush's interest in baseball never dwindled. He cheered mostly for the Houston Astros, whom he had watched as a young congressman from Texas in the

Bush takes a turn at the plate during a softball game at Kennebunkport, Maine, in the summer of 1989. (WIDE WORLD)

1960s. A high point came in 1983, when Bush attended an old-timers game in Denver, and pitcher Warren Spahn, one of baseball's all-time greats, persuaded Bush to put on a uniform and actually take part in the contest. "Gosh, I haven't swung a bat in years," Bush protested. But Spahn managed to persuade him to take the field before 34,000 screaming fans.

When it came his turn at bat, Spahn was on the mound. "He put one straight down the middle and I flailed away and popped it straight up in the air, first pitch," Bush recalled. An inning later, Bush came up to the plate a second time. Facing Milt Pappas, who won over 200 games in a major league career that ended in 1973, Bush rapped out a clean single to center field.

Bush was once asked by *Sports Illustrated* whether he envied those teammates and opponents who went on to play in the big leagues. "Oh, yes, I used to imagine how great it would be to stride up to the plate in a major league ballpark," Bush replied. "But by then my sights were set on doing something else. Still, baseball has always been a great love."

In a drawer of his desk at the Oval Office, Bush kept the first baseman's mitt he had used at Yale. Nearly fifty years old, it had been oiled, rewebbed, and carefully cared for, and looked in first-class condition. Bush once showed the glove to Thomas Boswell, a writer for the *Washington Post*. "It's the George McQuinn claw," the President explained to Boswell, putting it on his hand and popping his fist into the pocket. " 'Trapper' it says here. It's a Rawlings. I remember when this glove came out. It was wonderful. I think they outlawed this cup [style of pocket]. But now you can use anything."

Dwight Eisenhower was as skilled a ballplayer as George

The Abilene, Kansas, high school baseball team of 1909. Dwight D. Eisenhower is in the front row, center. (WIDE WORLD)

Bush. He patroled the outfield for his high school team in Abilene, Kansas. One season Eisenhower led the club in hitting and fielding.

One of Eisenhower's sharpest baseball memories was not a happy one. His high school squad was playing a team made up of freshmen from Kansas University. Practically the entire town had turned out to see whether the local youngsters could defeat the older, more experienced players. The game was a tight pitching duel, with Abilene clinging to a 1–0 lead going into the ninth inning. The university team got a runner on first base, and then their most powerful slugger came to the plate to punch a line drive over second base. Eisenhower, in center field, hurried in to make the catch. But the ball kept rising. Eisenhower hesitated for a split second, then realized he had misjudged the ball. He started to backpedal. But it was too late. The ball soared over his upstretched glove and rolled toward the fence. By the time Eisenhower retrieved the ball and threw it in, the batter had rounded the bases. The hit resulted in a 2–1 win for the university squad. Eisenhower, blaming himself for the loss, was dejected.

William Howard Taft enjoyed baseball both as a fan and a player. He sometimes attended two games in the same day. As a young man, Taft played second base for the Mount Auburn team in Cincinnati. He was a solid fielder with an accurate arm and also provided power at the plate. Taft's failing was that he had no speed and could only lumber about the bases.

Theodore Roosevelt was prevented from playing baseball because he had to wear glasses. Once, after watching his son Quentin play the game, he wrote: "I like to see Quentin practicing baseball. It gives me hope that one of my boys will not take after his father in this respect and be able to play the national game!"

CHAPTER 10

LOOKING
BACK

Golfing is bill clinton's favorite sport. george Bush golfed, too, and also played tennis. Jimmy Carter was another tennis player; he also played softball. Bush was a first baseman in college, and he occasionally attended baseball games during his presidential term. Ronald Reagan, Richard Nixon, Gerald Ford, and Dwight Eisenhower were college football players.

All of these presidents enjoyed sports that have one thing in common: They are of fairly recent origin. In the times of George Washington, John Adams, and the other early presidents, today's most popular sports didn't even exist. There was no baseball, football, hockey, skiing, or golf. Basketball and volleyball hadn't been invented. There were no track-and-field meets. The modern Olympic Games didn't begin until 1896, almost a century after George Washington had died.

Many people, however, enjoyed sports, both as participants and spectators. It's just that sports were casual and informal. Most games were pickup affairs, organized on the

An early form of baseball. (NEW YORK PUBLIC LIBRARY)

spur of the moment, when boys met in an open field or village green to choose up sides. (Girls almost never participated in vigorous outdoor sports in those days. They remained at home, learning to cook, sew, and do the other tasks it took to be a "good wife.")

They played several ball and bat games, including cricket, rounders, and stool ball, all of which resembled baseball. A batter tried to hit a pitched ball. If he did hit it, he ran to a base. If he hit a fly ball and it was caught, he was out.

Such games were played more frequently in the Northeast than in other parts of the country. In the Northeast, people were more likely to live in cities or towns, where there were greater opportunities for boys to join together to form teams and compete.

John Adams, who was elected in 1797 as the nation's second president, played early versions of soccer and baseball. The oldest of a family of three boys, John Adams was short and slender. As a youngster, he was always on the run and eager to take part in any kind of sports or physical activities. He swam in the summer and skated in the winter. He bowled, flew kites, boxed, and wrestled. The family had a farm in the town of Braintree, about ten miles south of Boston, and young John would ride one of the farm horses whenever he got a chance. The horses were big, heavy, and thickly muscled, quite unlike the sleek saddle horses ridden by George Washington and other Virginia planters. And there was no fancy saddle for young John. He would ride bareback across the vast meadowlands.

Soccer—then called football—came to the colonies with the earliest settlers. But the sport played by young John Adams scarcely resembled the game played today. Often the ball was a leather bag stuffed with rags or sawdust. An open field or empty road served as a playing area. There were no written rules. Any number of players could make up a side. There were no goals, no scoring. The idea was simply to advance the ball by kicking it in one direction or another. It was great fun, with some players leading the way while others struggled to keep up with the pack. Loud shrieks and whoops of laughter filled the air.

The simplicity of the game helped to make it very popular. It got *too* popular, in fact: The citizens of some towns came to look upon the sport as a nuisance. The people of Boston passed a law that stated: "Football is not to be played at, or kicked at, through any part of the town."

The bat-and-ball game that John Adams played as a boy was often called rounders. Like soccer, it had been imported from England. The bat was a paddle or slim fencepost. The ball, about the size of the one used in the game of softball today, had a leather cover and was stuffed with horsehair. Players did not use gloves.

The object of rounders was the same as that of modern baseball—to score runs by hitting a ball and running around the bases. In New England, the game was sometimes called town ball because it was played on the village green by young boys while their fathers attended town hall meetings.

Legend has it that John Adams, at age fourteen, was playing rounders one day when his father called him from the field to tell him that he wasn't spending enough time at his studies. If he planned to enter Harvard, he would have to change his ways, his father said. Rounders would have to become less important in his life.

Adams must have taken his father's advice, for the next year, not long before his sixteenth birthday, John entered Harvard with the freshman class. Some of the college rules and regulations saddened him. One said he could not keep a rifle. John knew that the woods and marshes near Harvard were filled with ducks, partridges, pheasants, rabbits, and squirrels, but for his four years as a student, he would not be able to hunt them. In addition, students were not permitted to fish in the Charles River, which bordered the campus.

The only recreation period of the day followed dinner, the heartiest meal of the day, which was served at noon and lasted until around two o'clock. It was John's custom to rush from the dinner table as soon as he had finished eating and hurry to the campus playing field, where a game of soccer or rounders was usually under way.

Harvard's rules of conduct apparently were not too great a burden for young John Adams. He had a splendid record there, and went on to become a lawyer, a member of the Massachusetts legislature, a delegate to both the First and Second Continental Congress, a diplomat, and the nation's first vice president, before becoming president.

IN THE SOUTH, WHERE THE POPULATION WAS SPREAD OUT, IT was different. There were few towns and few opportunities for boys to meet and play games.

In much of the South, the land was divided into plantations. These were enormous estates made up of vast forests and cultivated farmland. In Virginia, Maryland, Kentucky, and North Carolina, tobacco was the chief crop. In South Carolina, Georgia, and the Gulf states, it was cotton.

Wealthy planters, such as George Washington, were avid sportsmen. The sports they enjoyed the most were foxhunting, horse racing, and cockfighting. These were also the sports most popular with the English nobility.

Washington's life as a Virginia planter began in 1759, when, aged twenty-seven, he married Martha Custis, a wealthy widow with two children. Two years later, he inherited Mount Vernon and its 2,000 acres. Washington expanded Mount Vernon, building major additions to the house and increasing his landholdings to almost 8,000 acres.

Nearby lived Lord Thomas Fairfax, an English-born nobleman. Fairfax was an enthusiastic sportsman. He liked foxhunting better than any other sport and taught Washington all he knew about it.

Foxhunting is a spine-tingling sport, one that involves courage, stamina, and great horsemanship. Foxhounds, in a pack, pursue the fox, while everyone follows on horseback. Riders have to be capable of traveling at breakneck speed,

Washington (left) points out the way for Lord Fairfax during a foxhunt. (AMERICAN MUSEUM OF NATURAL HISTORY)

avoiding trees, rocks, and other obstacles, and jumping over fences and walls and across ditches and streams. The chase is what it's all about. The fox is not shot, but killed by the hounds.

In Virginia, the foxhunting season lasted from November to March. During that time, Mount Vernon was usually crowded with relatives and friends of the Washingtons who came from near and far. Visits lasted for weeks at a time.

Guests at Mount Vernon hunted three times a week. They would be awakened before dawn and served a breakfast of corncakes and milk by candlelight. By sunrise, the hunt had begun and would last for several hours. Afterward, dinner was served at the mansion house, where toasts would be offered to the boldest rider and fastest hound.

On such occasions, Washington wore the finest clothes—a blue coat, scarlet waistcoat, buckskin breeches, and velvet cap. He usually rode to the hounds on Blueskin, a speedy animal with great endurance. Washington named the horse for its dark, metallic-gray coat, which sometimes took on a bluish hue. "Washington rode," wrote George W. Parke Custis, his step-grandson, "as he did everything, with ease, elegance, and with power . . . and ridiculed the idea of its being even possible that he should be unhorsed, providing the animal kept on its legs."

Describing a hunt at Mount Vernon, Custis wrote: "There were roads cut through the woods in various directions, by which the aged or timid riders, or ladies, could enjoy the exhilarating cry, without the risk of life or limb, but Washington rode gaily up to his hounds, through all difficulties and dangers on the grounds on which he hunted."

In his diaries, Washington kept track of the number of times he went foxhunting and described what happened on each occasion. One entry reads: "Went a Huntg and killed a Fox, after treeing him in 35 minutes." Another time, he wrote: "Went a Hunting after breakfast and Found a Fox at Muddy Hole and killed her . . . after a chace of better than two hours, and treeing her twice, the last of which times she fell dead out of the Tree." (Notice that Washington misspelled the word "chase." He was not a good speller, nor was he skilled in the forms and uses of words.)

Washington enjoyed the contented life of a Virginia planter until 1775, when the American Revolution began

George Washington was a skilled horseman from a very early age. Here he is pictured on a military mission in 1754. (LIBRARY OF CONGRESS)

and he was chosen as commander in chief of the Continental Army. Eight years passed before the English were defeated, the new nation born, and Washington, then in his fifties, returned to Mount Vernon.

Thomas Jefferson, James Madison, and James Monroe were other presidents who were born and brought up in Virginia and owned plantations. Jefferson, like Washington, was a skilled horseman who enjoyed fishing and hunting, but not with the enthusiasm of his friend George Washington.

✢   ✢   ✢

IN THE EARLY DAYS OF OUR NATION, HUNTING AND FISHING were not merely pleasant outdoor activities. For people who lived in rural areas or on the frontier, hunting and fishing were a way of life, the means of providing the game, fish, and fowl that were needed for family meals.

Being a marksman was not only a source of pride, it cut down on the amount of ammunition one needed. James Buchanan, the oldest of eleven children, hunted in the forests of Pennsylvania as a youth. He was such a good shot he considered it a disgrace to bring home a squirrel unless he had brought the animal down with a single shot directly through its head.

Since virtually all men were skilled with a rifle, shooting matches were popular. The typical Kentucky rifle of the day weighed about eight pounds, was almost five feet long, and fired a lead ball that was close to half an inch in diameter.

Frontier marksmen could perform uncanny feats with the Kentucky rifle (which actually originated in Pennsylvania). They could drive a nail straight into a tree with a rifle ball or, using a knife blade as a target, slice a ball into two equal pieces.

Frontier sports were different from the sports popular in the East. In the Ohio country, Illinois, Indiana, Kentucky, and Tennessee, contests that stressed physical strength and man-to-man competition were what prevailed. Wrestling was one of them. In those days, a wrestler won a match merely by throwing his opponent to the ground. He did not have to pin the man's shoulders to the ground to be declared the winner.

Many frontier sports were similar to modern-day track-

and-field events. These included foot races, the broad jump, and weightlifting. Throwing the long bullet, an iron ball that weighed several pounds, was also popular. The long bullet was thrown from a leather sling to make it land so as to roll toward a marked goal.

Abraham Lincoln, tall and lanky as a boy, had few opportunities to take part in sports in remote Hardin County, Kentucky, where he was born. "There was about one human being to each square mile," Lincoln later wrote.

After the family moved to Spencer County, Indiana, Abe worked as a farmhand. At seventeen, he was more than six feet tall and as strong as or stronger than any of the older men who worked with him. It was said young Abe could dead-lift 400 pounds with relative ease; he was also said to have once lifted 600 pounds. One witness said Lincoln could "sink an ax deeper than any man I ever saw."

Wrestling was one of Lincoln's favorite sports. In friendly matches, he threw anyone who was bold enough to challenge him. When the family moved to Macon County, Illinois, in 1830, when Lincoln was twenty-one, his reputation as a wrestler followed him. In nearby Cumberland County, tough, young Dan Needham was the champion wrestler. Needham heard about Lincoln's wrestling accomplishments and boasted, "I can fling that young upstart any day of the week."

The two eventually met at a match staged at Wabash Point. Both men were six foot four, slim, and well-muscled. According to a Lincoln biographer, Carl Sandburg, they resembled a pair of panthers. But young Abe was much stronger than his opponent. They grappled four times, and each time Lincoln quickly and easily sent Needham to the ground. It happened so fast that Needham's pride was in-

Tall and well muscled, Abraham Lincoln won renown as a rail-splitter — and wrestler. (NEW YORK PUBLIC LIBRARY)

jured and he challenged Lincoln to a fistfight. Lincoln, keeping his good humor, managed to talk Needham out of it.

Not long after this incident, Lincoln took a job as a clerk
in a general store in New Salem, Illinois, owned by Denton
Offut. Offut liked to boast that his clerk could "outrun, out-
fit, outwrestle and throw down any man in Sangamon
County." And Offut offered to support his man with a hefty
bet. Bill Clary, who ran a saloon next door, heard Offut's
boast and accepted the wager. The saloonkeeper's choice to
defeat Lincoln was Jack Armstrong, short and very powerful, and the leader of the troublesome Clary's Grove Boys,
who lived about four miles away.

On the day of the match, held in an empty lot next to
Offut's store, spectators came from as far as fifty miles away.
The Clary's Grove Boys turned out in force and backed their
man with bets of money, knives, and whiskey.

At the referee's signal, the two men, who had stripped to
the waist, circled each other cautiously. Armstrong kept trying to get in close and seize Lincoln in a deadly hold. But
the taller Lincoln kept fending him off with his long arms.
The two men grappled, broke, then grappled and broke
again.

Little by little, Lincoln began wearing Armstrong down.
The stockier man began gasping for breath. Lincoln suddenly made his move, wrapping his arms around Armstrong's head. As Lincoln increased the pressure of the
headlock, Armstrong fouled Lincoln by stamping on Abe's
instep with a heavy boot.

Infuriated, Lincoln retaliated. He reached out and
grasped Armstrong by the throat, lifted him into the air,
shook him like a rag doll, then slammed him to the ground.
Armstrong lay flat on his back, dazed and utterly defeated.

Shocked at the outcome, the Clary's Grove Boys swarmed about Lincoln, shouting threats. But Lincoln did not flinch. He declared he was willing to fight them all one at a time. But before any blows were struck, Armstrong, back on his feet, broke through the mob to shake Lincoln's hand and shout to his supporters that Lincoln had won fairly. "He's the best feller that ever broke into this settlement," Armstrong declared.

After that, Lincoln became a hero to the Clary's Grove Boys. They called on him to judge their wrestling matches, horse races, and cockfights.

When he was twenty-three Lincoln enlisted in the militia to fight in the war against Chief Black Hawk, leader of the Sauk and Fox tribe. He continued to add to his reputation as a wrestling champion. After he was made captain of the Illinois volunteers, his men declared that no one in the army could outwrestle Captain Abe.

Lorenzo Thompson, a well-known wrestler from Union County, challenged Lincoln. A championship bout, the winner to take two out of three falls, was arranged. One look at Thompson and Lincoln knew he was in for a rugged time. His opponent was very tall, almost as tall as Lincoln himself, heavily muscled, with wide shoulders and bulging thighs. Thompson's size didn't bother Lincoln's backers. They bet heavily on their Captain Abe.

When the two wrestlers met, and grappled and separated for the first time, Lincoln's worries were confirmed. He glanced at his friends in the crowd and said, "Boys, this is the most powerful man I ever had a hold of."

The two men grappled again. Then Thompson suddenly seized Lincoln in a "crotch hoist" and slammed him to the ground to win the first fall.

With Lincoln back on his feet, the wrestlers circled, feinted, and grappled. Then Thompson got Lincoln in his grasp again. As Abe was going down he reached out and grabbed Thompson and dragged him down with him. Both men lay stretched out.

Lincoln's backers shouted the second fall should be declared a draw since neither man had been thrown cleanly. But Thompson's supporters argued that their man had thrown Lincoln for a second time, and thus had won the match. Tempers flared and a free-for-all threatened to erupt. Abe raised a hand and faced the angry crowd. "Boys, give up your bets," he shouted to his supporters. "If this man has not thrown me fairly, he could have." Lincoln's friends paid off what they owed, but they would not concede that Captain Abe had been defeated. Years later, Lincoln admitted Thompson had thrown him, adding, "He could have thrown a grizzly bear."

In the decades following the Civil War, the United States went through a period of enormous change. Immigrants from northern and western Europe poured into the country. Most of them settled in big cities. Industry and agriculture benefited from the use of labor-saving machines. More leisure time for Americans was one result.

Sports surged in popularity. Professional baseball teams were organized in scores of American cities, and in 1876 teams from eight cities established the National League of Professional Baseball Clubs (which is, simply, the National League today).

The U.S. Lawn Tennis Association was founded in 1881, the U.S. Golf Association in 1894, and the American Bowl-

Organized sports surged in popularity during the 1880s and 1890s. Here Princeton faces Yale in football, 1889. (NEW YORK PUBLIC LIBRARY)

ing Congress in 1895. Basketball was invented in 1891 and was soon being played in every part of the country.

American presidents started doing what everyone else was doing. They still fished, hunted, and went horseback riding, of course. But before the end of the century, they were also golfing and playing tennis, and presidents-to-be were demonstrating their skills on the baseball diamond or had become the game's fans.

Many different sports are important today, but often for different reasons. "There is an aura around people who succeed and compete successfully and who are physically fit," said Robert Schleser, co-director of the Center of Sport and Performance Psychology at Chicago's Illinois Institute of

Technology, in 1993. "It's a 'halo effect' that causes them to be perceived as more credible, more trustworthy, more knowledgeable."

Bill Clinton, who jogs and plays golf, George Bush, who never met a sport he didn't like, and Ronald Reagan, with his riding and wood-chopping, all seemed to be pursuing that goal.

APPENDIX

The Presidents and Their Sports

PRESIDENT	TERM	HT.	WT.	SPORTS
Bill Clinton (1946–)	1993–	6'2"	205 lb.	Golf, jogging, bowling
George Bush (1924–)	1989–1993	6'2"	190 lb.	Tennis, golf, horseshoes, fishing, hunting, speedboating, softball
Ronald Reagan (1911–)	1981–1989	6'1"	190 lb.	Riding, swimming, calisthenics
Jimmy Carter (1924–)	1977–1981	5'9"	170 lb.	Jogging, tennis, fishing, softball, skiing, bicycling
Gerald Ford (1913–)	1974–1977	6'	195 lb.	Golf, skiing, swimming, jogging
Richard Nixon (1913–1994)	1969–1974	5'11"	175 lb.	Golf, walking, bowling
Lyndon Baines Johnson (1908–1973)	1963–1969	6'	190 lb.	Swimming, speedboating, walking, golf, riding
John F. Kennedy (1917–1963)	1961–1963	6'	170 lb.	Swimming, golf, touch football, sailing, softball
Dwight D. Eisenhower (1890–1969)	1953–1961	5'11"	175 lb.	Golf, hunting, fishing, riding, skeet shooting

PRESIDENT	TERM	HT.	WT.	SPORTS
Harry S. Truman (1884–1972)	1945–1953	5'9"	170 lb.	Walking, fishing, horseshoes
Franklin D. Roosevelt (1882–1945)	1933–1945	6'2"	185 lb.	Swimming, fishing, sailing, rowing
Herbert Hoover (1874–1964)	1929–1933	5'11"	185 lb.	Medicine ball, fishing
Calvin Coolidge (1872–1933)	1923–1929	5'10"	165 lb.	Fishing, hunting, riding, walking, skeet shooting
Warren G. Harding (1865–1923)	1921–1923	6'	200 lb.	Golf, riding, table tennis, tennis
Woodrow Wilson (1856–1924)	1913–1921	5'11"	175 lb.	Golf, walking, riding
William Howard Taft (1857–1930)	1909–1913	6'	310 lb.	Golf, riding
Theodore Roosevelt (1858–1919)	1901–1909	5'10"	170 lb.	Tennis, golf, hunting, fishing, polo, boxing, wrestling, jujitsu, riding, walking, mountain climbing

Name	Term	Height	Weight	Activities
William McKinley (1843–1901)	1897–1901	5'7"	165 lb.	Fishing, riding, swimming, golf, walking
Benjamin Harrison (1833–1901)	1889–1893	5'6"	140 lb.	Hunting, fishing, ice skating
Grover Cleveland (1837–1908)	1885–1889 1893–1897	5'11"	260 lb.	Fishing, hunting
Chester Alan Arthur (1830–1886)	1881–1885	6'2"	225 lb.	Fishing, hunting, swimming
James A. Garfield (1831–1881)	1881	6'	185 lb.	Riding, walking, billiards
Rutherford B. Hayes (1822–1893)	1877–1881	5'9"	170 lb.	Hunting, croquet
Ulysses S. Grant (1822–1885)	1869–1877	5'9"	165 lb.	Riding, swimming, ice skating
Andrew Johnson (1808–1875)	1865–1869	5'10"	175 lb.	None
Abraham Lincoln (1809–1865)	1861–1865	6'4"	180 lb.	Wrestling, walking, weightlifting, billiards, bowling
James Buchanan (1791–1868)	1857–1861	6'	180 lb.	Hunting, walking

PRESIDENT	TERM	HT.	WT.	SPORTS
Franklin Pierce (1804–1869)	1853–1857	5'10"	170 lb.	Swimming, walking
Millard Fillmore (1800–1874)	1850–1853	5'9"	175 lb.	None
Zachary Taylor (1784–1850)	1849–1850	5'8"	170 lb.	Hunting, riding, swimming
James K. Polk (1795–1849)	1845–1849	5'8"	140 lb.	None
John Tyler (1790–1862)	1841–1845	6'	170 lb.	Riding
William Henry Harrison (1773–1841)	1841	5'8"	145 lb.	Riding
Martin Van Buren (1782–1862)	1837–1841	5'6"	135 lb.	Riding, walking

Name	Term	Height	Weight	Sports
Andrew Jackson (1767–1845)	1829–1837	6'1"	150 lb.	Riding
John Quincy Adams (1767–1848)	1825–1829	5'7"	170 lb.	Riding, swimming, walking, billiards
James Monroe (1758–1831)	1817–1825	6'	185 lb.	Hunting, riding, fishing, swimming
James Madison (1751–1836)	1809–1817	5'4"	100 lb.	Walking
Thomas Jefferson (1743–1826)	1801–1809	6'2"	180 lb.	Riding, fishing, swimming, walking
John Adams (1735–1826)	1797–1801	5'7"	170 lb.	Riding, hunting, swimming, ice skating
George Washington (1732–1799)	1789–1797	6'2"	175 lb.	Riding, foxhunting, hunting, fishing, billiards

INDEX

Note: Page numbers in italics refer to photographs.